New Wine: New Wineskins

Exploring the RCIA

New Wine: New Wineskins
Exploring the RCIA

James B. Dunning

An NCDD Book

William H. Sadlier, Inc.
Chicago
New York
Los Angeles

New Wine: New Wineskins

James B. Dunning
An NCDD Book

Nihil Obstat
Rev. David E. Beebe
Censor Deputatus

Imprimatur
Rev. Msgr. John F. Donoghue
Vicar General for the Archdiocese of Washington

February 18, 1981

The nihil obstat and imprimatur are official declarations that a book or pamphlet is free of doctrinal or moral error. No implication is containted therein that those who have granted the nihil obstat and imprimatur agree with the contents, opinions, or statements expressed.

Acknowledgments
Excerpt from THE SEASONS OF A MAN'S LIFE, by Daniel Levinson.
Copyright © 1978 by Daniel Levinson.
Reprinted by permission of Alfred A. Knopf, Inc.

Excerpts from WIND, SAND AND STARS by Antoine de Saint-Exupery is reprinted by permission of Harcourt Brace Jovanovic, Inc.

Reprinted with permission of Macmillan Publishing, Co., Inc.
from LETTERS AND PAPERS FROM PRISON by Dietrich Bonhoeffer.
Copyright © 1953, 1967, 1971 by SCM Press, Ltd.

Excerpt from A PASSION PLAY by Catherine de Vinck.
All Rights Reserved, Catherine de Vinck, 1975.

ISBN: 0-8215-9807-4
Library of Congress Catalog Card Number: 80-54708
    4 5 6 7 8 9 / 9 8 7 6 5 4 3
Published by
William H. Sadlier, Inc.
11 Park Place
New York, New York 10007

Table of Contents

# Foreword

A mere fifteen years has passed since the conclusion of Vatican II in 1965, yet its impact over these years on the life and direction of the Roman Catholic Church has been enormous. The thrust of its reform has touched every facet of Catholic life, most notably those which deal with catechesis and liturgy.

One avenue of reform which has opened up new horizons within the Church today is the restoration of the catechumenate. Since the promulgation of the *Rite of Christian Initiation of Adults* (RCIA) in 1972, and a provisional English text published in 1974 by the United States Catholic Conference, much has been written about its impact and pastoral application across the land. In the meantime, in-depth workshops have been held, catechumenates have been established, pastors and parishioners have been deeply affected by the roles they play in welcoming, nurturing and celebrating the entrance of new adult members into their faith community.

The National Conference of Diocesan Directors of Religious Education-CCD (NCDD) first gave its attention to this document and its ramifications during the 1976 annual meeting held in Boston under the title "Catechumenate: Catechesis: Community." The planning committee of that same conference foresaw the potential use of RCIA by diocesan directors in addressing contemporary structures of catechesis, liturgy and adult religious education. Some participants even predicted a model which would have implications for the future shape of parish catechesis.

In 1980, the membership of NCDD requested further attention be given to the broad topic of the catechumenate and its potential impact on parishes. When they chose as the priority topic for an annual resource paper,"The RCIA: Its Implications for Parish Catecheis," it was quite natural for NCDD to ask Rev. James B. Dunning to write such a paper. As a prominent speaker and author in this area of research, Father Dunning was eminently qualified to explore such a topic. He has served as Director of Continuing Education in the Archdiocese of Seattle and now holds the post of Executive Director of the National Conference of Continuing Education of Roman Catholic Clergy. He also is coeditor of a new quarterly professional journal, *Christian Initiation Resources,* and participated in the International Symposium on Christian Initiation held in France in 1978.

In *New Wine: New Wineskins* Father Dunning opens with a brief historical survey of the catechumenate, and then describes the stages of the catechumenal process and its implications on parish life. With pastoral concerns upper most in his mind, he places great emphasis on the concept of growing in faith and on how parishioners can be a part of the faith development of others. He also highlights the impact that the catechumenal process has on current sacramental catechesis.

The NCDD salutes Father Dunning for his pioneering contribution to the contemporary catechetical endeavor. It is only by continued research such as his that the RCIA will become a vibrant reality in parish communities across the country. The NCDD equally commends William H. Sadlier, Inc., for taking the initiative in fostering the study of the RCIA and its implications for parish catechesis.

In the decade that lies ahead, the reforms of Vatican II will continue to be implemented. The restoration of the catechumenate can serve as a vehicle for Catholics old and new to grow in and to deepen their faith as they continue to live as believers in the Lord.

David E. Beebe
Executive Secretary, NCDD

 **Introduction**

The new *Rite of Christian Initiation of Adults* (RCIA) of 1972 is one of the best kept secrets since Vatican Council II.

For some it denotes an ominous department of the American intelligence community. For others it is just one more document, written in the dry language of "Vaticanese," imposed on us by the rite-makers after the Council. Still others claim either it is one more archaism based on the principle that "old means better," or it is obviously written for missionary countries and not for lands supposedly firm in faith (as if the Church could ever be not-on-mission).

Perhaps others intuitively sense that this rite confronts our most fundamental assumptions about Church and with good reason keep their distance. Perhaps they sense that the RCIA is indeed new wine.

> No one patches up an old coat with a piece of new cloth, for the new patch will shrink and make an even bigger hole in the coat. Nor does anyone pour new wine into used wineskins, for the skins will burst, the wine will pour out, and the skins will be ruined. Instead, new wine is poured into fresh wineskins, and both will keep in good condition.

> (Matthew 9:16-17)

Too often we have tinkered with other reforms since Vatican Council II. We have pasted and patched together rites of Reconciliation and Eucharist. But the wine of RCIA is too strong. If it is poured into the wineskins of a Church which ministers only through priests and initiates primarily through doctrine, the ecclesiastical bags will burst.

The old wineskins were well captured in the title of a catechism much used in the mid-twentieth century, *Father Smith Instructs Jackson*. The model was the familiar inquiry class, and the primary goal was instruction in Catholic teaching. The RCIA is about conversion, about the spiritual journey of the whole person (not just the cortex) to God. It is the fine wine of journeying to God in community, not just the diet soda of instruction. Even more. It is initiation into a community of believers, not just an introduction to Father Smith. If Father Smith no longer instructs Jackson but tries to evangelize, catechize, illuminate, and celebrate Jackson (the four periods in the RCIA), both Father Smith and Jackson will burst. The RCIA is the most radical document since Vatican II because it sends us back to our roots in being Church. The entire community is the new wineskins. The RCIA calls the entire community into mission, into sharing both Good News and their personal faith in the Lord. That is what is so exciting. That is also what is so depressing. Where are all these communities and Christians aglow with the wine of the Spirit?

That may be why Ralph Keifer writes: "This is a revolution quite without precedent because the Catholic Church has never before in its history done such violence to its liturgical practice as to make its rites so thoroughly incongruous with its concrete reality. A step like this is either a statement that rite is wholly irrelevant or that the church is willing to change and to change radically its concrete reality. Such an approach is either suicide or prophecy of the highest order."[1] That may be why the RCIA is the best kept secret since Vatician II.

Some folks, in small pockets throughout this land, have tasted this new wine and liked it.

A catechumen:

The first thing I learned was that I wasn't alone in my questions and searching. I met good people who besides sharing questions helped each other find new meaning and purpose to life and religion. The catechumenate was great, not because it gave me something I didn't have, but because it helped me find the God who was with me all along and helped me respond to God.

Sister Jean Tranel, a catechumenate director:

The enthusiasm and hope generated by the people in the program are overwhelming. From my personal experience, it surpasses anything that I have worked with. The depth of community building is an experience that no other renewal program has achieved.[2]

Ray Kemp, a pastor:

The parish is charged with a new hospitality, an openness that was always there but not always viewed as a ministry. Evangelization is just a word unless parishes restore the catechumenate. The liturgical seasons of Lent and Easter are "let's pretend" times without the elect and the neophyte. Parishes that are not joining new members to their community around the table of the Lord are hiding the light that searches out the darkness, the healing spirit that challenges while it sooths.[3]

Bishop Maurice Dingman of Des Moines:

I would characterize the Christian community in my diocese as a "slumbering giant".... New attitudes have been formed in accordance with Vatican II documents. But there is little awareness of the potentiality that resides in that faith community.... What is needed is an awakening of this "slumbering giant." I suggest that the RCIA is the explosive bomb that can alert the faith community to its potentiality for evangelization.[4]

In my experience, those who have tried to enflesh the process described in the RCIA are charged with a similar delight and enthusiasm.

For those who would try a similar incarnation, the basic text is the RCIA itself, especially the Introduction. Based upon the experiences of many other people whom I met at the International Symposium on the Catechumenate in France, 1978, and in parishes and workshops through this country, plus research, this book for the most part will take a pastoral direction which will try to help translate theory and document into practice. It includes:

1. a very brief history of Christian Initiation;
2. some assumptions about the process involved in the RCIA;
3. pastoral suggestions for each of the four periods of the RCIA;
4. implications of the RCIA for some other dimensions of ministry.

Before beginning, you might spend some time with Figure 1 which gives an overview of the terminology and progression of the new RCIA. In the Spirit of the RCIA, it would also do no harm to read while sipping WINE.

FIGURE #1

1st Period	1st Stage	2nd Period	2nd Stage	3rd Period	3rd Stage	4th Period
Precatechumenate Inquiry	Entrance into Catechumenate	Catechumenate	Call and Selection	Illumination	Sacraments of Initiation	Mystagogia
Unlimited		One to a Few Years		Lent		Paschal Time
Personal Story Questions of Meaning Evangelization Initial Conversion	First Welcome into Church	Deepen Faith in Living Community, and Through Church Tradition	Admisssion to Those Elected for Initiation	Spiritual Direction Purification Preparation for Sacraments	Full Initiation into Church	Deepening of Sacramental Life and Choice of Service or Ministries
"Inquirers"		"Catechumens"		"Elect"		"Neophytes"
Awakening of Faith		Deepening of Faith Through Community		Discernment of Faith and Levels of Conversion		Celebration of Faith and Sharing Faith in Ministries
No Specific Rite Prayers Suggested	Rite of Becoming a Catechumen	Celebrations of Word; Minor Exorcisms; Blessings (Optional: Presentations of Creed, Lord's Prayer; Prayer over Ears, Mouth; Anointing)	Rite of Election	Scrutinies Presentations of Creed, Lord's Prayer; Pre-Vigil Rites	Baptism Confirmation Eucharist	Sunday Eucharists Celebrations; Eucharist with Bishop; Anniversary Celebration

1. History of Christian Initiation

This will be a very cursory overview.[5] For those of us accustomed to inquiry classes in rectory basements, formation by book not community, and the whole endeavor given over to a professional like "Father Smith instructing Jackson," one of the lessons of history most difficult to comprehend is that in the Church of the first centuries those who initiated, welcomed, and journeyed with people to Christ and the Christian community were ordinary folks. They were ordinary people, who saw themselves as Church, and who saw Church as missionary—founded and grounded on and enlivened by a mission to share Good News.

Before there was a catechumenate, there were sponsors—a sponsoring, welcoming community of people who were convinced that Jesus was Good News for them and that he might be Good News for others. From the year 30 to 180, there was no catechumenal institution as such. Centuries before Guttenberg there were no catechisms. There were only Christians, sharing their lives, and sharing both the stories of Jesus and their own faith stories with other people. Before there was a program, there was a Church, a community. In a sense, before there was a Church, there was a mission, a mission to share Good News which created Church. And before there was a mission, there was a gift—the Good News of the enduring presence of the Risen Lord in his people.

Questions: can we glean from this very early history some hints about the qualities of people who might do the welcoming today? Some hints on how to initiate the initiators into their own personal experience of gift, mission, community?

From the year 180 and throughout the third century, the gift and mission experienced by the community emerged into more concrete expressions. There were pressures coming from the many heresies of that period plus the threat of persecution. There arose spontaneously small communities of Christians who gathered round the new members to strengthen their faith in various ways and support them in living the Christian life. These new members were called catechumens and the first threshold they crossed in the process of initiation was entrance into the catechumenate. Their period of formation in these catechumenal communities lasted three years on the average. If at the end of that time there were signs of real conversion, they crossed a second threshold: admission to baptism.

Catechumen was not the only term applied to them. There were other terms more suited to the various stages of their journey. Most expressed an action—auditors (those who are listening), elect (those who are chosen), those who are being enlightened, those who ask together, proselyte of Christ (one who is going towards Christ). Ministry from the community responded to the needs at these various stages of the journey.

Questions: given our own forms of "heresies" and "persecution" of Christian values, can a person believe and live the Gospel without the support of a strong "catechumenal" community? Do we live in an anti-Gospel age in which individuals could not enter nor grow in the Church without more than a "little help from our friends"? Given the various needs of the person on his/her journey of faith, could any one person, e.g., the priest, touch all the areas that need healing and new life? I stress that these are just questions. The reason that France, the eldest daughter of the Church, restored the Catechumenate process, however, was that she discovered she was "France pagan," caught in an anti-Christian, post-Christian, often Marxist milieu.

16

How many "ism's" in the United States eat away at genuine, Gospel Catholicism?

In the fourth and fifth centuries, on the one hand the catechumenate declined and on the other hand there was a renewal of baptismal preparations.

After Constantine, Christianity was "in," part of the system, and began to decline into a "non-prophet" organization. At the first threshold of the entrance to the catechumenate, people began to enter to gain social advantages, without conversion. Consequently, they would put off their baptism and absent themselves from instruction.

Paradoxically, that development strengthened the immediate preparation for Baptism. The Church created a brief but serious catechumenate during Lent, with continuing catechesis during Easter week.

However, the renewal was short-lived. The seven week period, brief though it was, was further reduced to three or four weeks. Inauthentic conversion and formalism also plagued this second threshold of preparation for Baptism; and by the end of the fifth century, the Lenten catechumenate had collapsed into empty forms. To show the extent of the decline, "reforms" included the Council of Braga which adopted a law requiring three weeks of preparation (572), Boniface in Germany in the eighth century who instructed catechumens for at least two months, and Alcuin who, when faced with the mass "conversions" prompted by Charlemagne, demanded a preparation of between seven and forty days.

Questions: even though we *may* live in an anti-Gospel time, do we still live in a Constantinian time when it is sometimes advantageous to join the Church for social reasons, e.g., before a marriage? Do some forms of our "civil religion" give blessing to the demons in American culture?[6] In view of conflicting values in America and the countless variation within individuals regarding their own personal values, can we march people lockstep through a nine-month program that happens to coincide efficiently with our scholastic year? Conversion is the issue, not time; but what are our assumptions regarding the length of time for conversion at this time in history?

17

We shall even more lightly skip over the next centuries. Some have suggested that infant Baptism is the cause for the disappearance of the catechumenate; but Michel Dujarier points out that while this did have an effect, there were still attempts to have parents of infants go through a baptismal preparation in stages. There were also some attempts with adults in mission lands. Over the centuries, the few signs of renewal generally happened in missionary efforts, culminating with Cardinal Lavigerie's efforts in Africa during the eighteenth century which involved stages of postulancy for two years, catechumenate for two years, and a major baptismal retreat. The giving of medals, rosaries, or crucifixes, however, marked the stages of the process rather than liturgical celebrations. That step was finally taken by the churches of Europe, as an immediate prod to the reforms of Vatican II.

Question: might a recovery of our vision of the Church as missionary stimulate our own most creative efforts at renewal?

This brief foray into history can set the context for some assumptions concerning Christian Initiation today.

2. Assumptions about the RCIA Process

I do not assert that all the following assumptions find a home between the lines of the RCIA. Some do. Others come from my own perceptions of rock-bottom foundations which ground Christian Initiation.

There are three sets of assumptions:

1. about the persons who journey in faith
2. about God, Christ, Church and ministries
3. about catechesis and liturgy

ABOUT PERSONS WHO JOURNEY IN FAITH

Paragraph 5 of the Rite sets the tone for the entire document:

"The rite of initiation is suited to the spiritual journey of adults, which varies according to the many forms of God's grace, the free cooperation of the individuals, the action of the Church, and the circumstances of time and place."

As a commentary on that paragraph there are the following assumptions.

1. About Persons

First, the Good News of Jesus proclaims the infinite value of every person, whose every hair is numbered and who is worth more than many sparrows (cf. Matthew 10), who has a unique spiritual journey full of fits and starts, agony and ecstacy, with wounds that cry for healing and with hopes and joys that call for thanksgiving, with dyings and risings. On the one hand, no package program truly honors that unique journey. On the other hand, the starting point of Christian Initiation is to cherish that life as God does with a faith that God is already present there.

Second, if such a person of infinite worth invites any of us to travel with her/him, all our processes and programs need to respect what we know about how adults grow and learn. This means the educational vision of a Malcolm Knowles, for example, with assumptions such as these: adults can be increasingly self-directive; learners are a rich resource for learning and their experience must be tapped, etc.[7] More importantly, it means the faith-vision that reflection upon a person's human experience is the entry point to discovering one's experience of the Lord. In Karl Rahner's pithy phrase, "The revelation of God to man is man."

Third, although there is tension between the good of persons and the good of the community, the healthiest persons are those who share hurts and joys in community; the healthiest communities are those which reverence the immense value of persons.[8] Many people have been so hurt by others that they are not only shy but scared stiff about sharing their personal journey. The RCIA assumes that healing can happen in community through the tender, loving care of a community of faith. That assumes extreme gentleness, respectful patience, warm hospitality, and deep faith which encourage persons to blossom in community.

2. About Journeying

First, let this be engraved upon the fleshy tablets of everyone's heart: Christian Initiation (and all of Christian growth, for that matter) is a *process not a program*! Perhaps the most frequent request from people implementing the RCIA is for model programs. I understand that rather task-oriented need. But in view of the preceding assumptions about the value and unique quality of every person's religious story, beware of squeezing large persons into tight packages.

I shall suggest later some dimensions of a process which grounds the four periods recommended by the RCIA.[9] I believe these dimensions parallel to some extent Bernard Lonergan's process of coming to insight: be attentive (tune your antennae into all the riches of your experience). Be reflective (plumb the meaning of all the data). Be responsible (be able-to-respond to what you discover). Be loving (share the gift with others).[10] Inquiry demands attention. Catechumenate demands reflection. Enlightenment demands response-ability. Mystagogia emerges from and into love.

Those are the four periods of RCIA. They overlap just as Lonergan's imperatives overlap. The point is that they are ingredients in a process of how persons grow; and because of their unique personal history, persons will move at their own rate through the process. For example, it may take months in the inquiry period to help persons get in touch with their experience and questions if they have been told for years that their experience was of no value. They have long ago ceased to "be attentive."

I know this complicates matters for busy ministers who groan at the prospect of a different program for every person-in-process. Thank God there are many similar routes traveled on different persons' journeys. Thank God also that experience has shown the Lord can bring forth remarkable changes, because the RCIA process itself creates remarkable openness in people. I simply assert that for years we have marched people through very "efficient" catechism programs. We have seen the fall-off of "converts" not converted. They learned a book but did not learn to integrate their unique life into the life of the community, their story into the larger story of Jesus and his people. Which in the long run is most "efficient"?

Second, there is an assumption that adult growth and conversion (or perhaps regression) are a *life-long process*.

Research in developmental psychology on stages of adult growth reveals old dogs do learn new tricks. Whereas Erik Erikson had just one stage of Generativity to mark the years be-

Figure #2

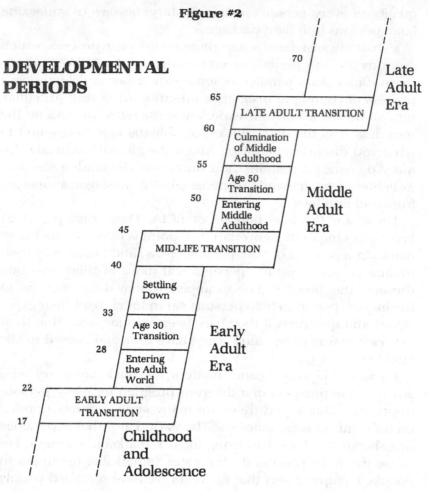

DEVELOPMENTAL PERIODS

70 — Late Adult Era

65

LATE ADULT TRANSITION

60

Culmination of Middle Adulthood

55

Age 50 Transition

50

Entering Middle Adulthood — Middle Adult Era

45

MID-LIFE TRANSITION

40

Settling Down

33

Age 30 Transition — Early Adult Era

28

Entering the Adult World

22

EARLY ADULT TRANSITION

17

Childhood and Adolescence

tween 25 and 65, studies by Roger Gould, Daniel Levinson and others indicate several crisis points during those years with new challenges and life tasks. For example, Levinson suggests that around 30 the men in his study looked back and raised questions about choices made of job and spouse during their busy 20s. About 40 they face their limits, begin to think of death, and raise questions about their future.[11] That may be why Carl Jung asserts, "Among all my patients in the second half of life—that is to say, over thirty-five—there has not been one whose problem in the last resort was not that of finding a religious

Figure #3

CONVERSIONS

TYPE	FROM	TO
1. AFFECTIVE	Blockage of Feelings	Acceptance and ability to use feelings
2. INTELLECTUAL	Knowledge as facts	Knowledge as meaning
3. MORAL	Satisfaction or Law as criteria of choices	Values as criteria of choices
4. RELIGIOUS Specified in:	Life as series of problems "one damn thing after another"	Life as mystery and gift
5. THEISTIC	God is a force	Personal relationship with God
6. CHRISTIAN	Historical Jesus	God's love for me in the living risen Christ
7. ECCLESIAL	Church is "They"/an institution	Church is "We"/a community

outlook on life."[12] All of this suggests some "teachable moments" when people might be looking at their lives and might enter deeper levels of both human growth and religious faith (cf. Figure 2).

Reflection on religious faith also reveals a spiritual journey which is life-long. We can agree with "born again" Christians that there may be a dramatic moment, a "fundamental option" reaching the deepest levels of our person and our values, a commitment from which most of our later choices and actions flow. Bernard Lonergan would call that "religious conversion"—the radical shift from seeing life as problem to seeing life as mystery and gift. Once that happens, however, the changes continue to touch and heal and release ever-deepening levels of our person. Edward Braxton has developed Lonergan's schema to include: affective conversion (from the blockage of feelings to release and ownership of feelings); intellectual conversion (from knowledge as measurable fact to meaning, mystery, wonder); moral conversion (from satisfaction or law to values as the criteria of choices); and specifications of religious conversion which include theistic (from God as impersonal force to loving Person); Christic (from the historical Jesus to Risen Lord who is God's love present to me); and ecclesial (from the church as "they" to the church as "we").[13] Conversion can be a jargon word; I have found these dimensions helpful in trying to assist people to discern where there are possibilities of change in their life-long journey (cf. Figure 3).

Certainly, assumptions in the RCIA include that God is personal, Jesus is risen, and the Church is "we."

Another assumption grounded on the belief that persons are on journey to the Lord is that the time of conversion is sacred time and the space is sacred space.

Nine-month or eighteen-month programs do not convert. God converts. Well-organized catechumenates that "put everyone in their place" do not convert. God in his sacred space converts. Programs can create an environment of curricula, meetings, schedules, and calendars. The time and space when each person meets God is outside time and space on that holy ground where one can discover that fire which burns with love and is not consumed. Even in "highly mobile America" (with pastors who claim you have to get them baptized before they move), we assume people need sacred time and space to journey into holy ground. Even in highly competitive America, one wine company assures us, "We will sell no wine before its time."

Journeying also leads to assumptions about adaptation.

First, this assumption is clear in the RCIA: because the person's spiritual journey is unique and because that journey also takes place in a specific cultural milieu—adapt, adapt, adapt.

What a joy to find a Roman document calling for creativity, flexibility, adaptability! (cf. *RCIA*, nos. 64-67).

Some have taken this to mean, "We need to adapt to culture. Everything educational in America happens in nine months. Even though the RCIA says 'the preparation of adults takes a long time' (n. 290), adapt." We have said enough on that! But adaptations of language and the shape of the rites, and adaptations to conversions in individuals which take place "without our permission"—that certainly is in order. A study by the Bishops' Committee on the Liturgy reveals a dearth of that kind of creative adaptation.

Second, the RCIA is primarily for new Catholic Christians; but the process can be adapted for old Catholic Christians. We are past the time when the bulletin announcement can read in September, "Inquiry class begins this Wednesday: all Catholics who wish to update their religion are also invited to attend." Certainly, in catechumenal communities, there are "old Catholics" acting as catechists and sponsors; but they are there for the catechumens. To dump 5 catechumens into a group of 30 Catholics who want to update themselves is to mix apples and oranges. The catechumens can get lost. As one catechumen said, "We spend our time discussing their baggage and hangups!" Now, catechumens need to be exposed to those "hangups." They have to live with these people next to them in the pews. But that should not dominate the process.

However, since the same process of deepening conversion holds true for new and old Catholics, we hope it will spread into general parish renewal. I am serving as a resource person in two parishes which have implemented the RCIA for new Catholics for three years. The "old timers" wanted in on the act, so the parish staffs designed a process which follows the progression of the RCIA for all the adults and also for family clusters. In one parish of 900 households, some 500 people participated; in the second parish, 60% of the adults have begun the process. But it is a separate track: these people are at a different point in their journey.

A third assumption is that not all of the so-called archaic language needs to be adapted. Test it with the people first. Some have concluded too quickly, I believe, that language like catechumen, neophyte, and mystagogia is obsolete. I suggest we try a re-cycling. In parishes which have implemented the RCIA it is surprising how quickly people have picked up the language; they seem to like it. Perhaps it is an experience of liminality: language and symbol from outside a culture can stimulate wonder. The term, mystagogia, for example, can also provide a catechetical moment. When someone asks, "What does that mean?", it gives us a chance to reflect upon the call of all of us after initiation to enter more deeply into the mysteries of the dying and rising of Jesus and into conversion as a life-long story.

3. About Faith

First, there is an assumption that the Protestants were right about biblical faith. Faith includes but is more than "intellectual assent to truths on the authority of God revealing" (Vatican I). Faith is the surrender of the whole person as a response to God's gift and presence in Christ Jesus.

Faith is personal *surrender*, commitment, decision. It is basic stance, attitude, and answer to God which comes before any words, doctrines, or theologies which express "the faith."

Faith involoves the *whole person*, on increasingly deepening levels of conversion. It is more than intellectual; and as the perceptive catechist has always known, learning the book "ain't" enough.

Faith is a *response*. Good News comes first. The gift of God in Christ Jesus comes first; then we answer.

Faith is a response to *God's gift and presence in Jesus*: it is a personal response to a Person, not just to doctrines about him. Christian faith involves religious conversion (life is gift), theistic (God is for-giving, the greatest gift), and Christic (Jesus is the presence of the gift of God).

Second, the RCIA assumes that normally faith is best nourished in community. It assumes ecclesial conversion which means that "we" all have stories of faith to share and that in those stories God in Christ Jesus becomes present to us. The RCIA puts it this way: "The initiation of catechumens takes place step by step in the midst of the community of the faithful. Together with the catechumens, the faithful reflect upon the value of the paschal mystery, renew their own conversion, and by their example lead the catechumens to obey the Holy Spirit more generously" (*RCIA*, n. 4).

For that reason, the process in the RCIA is very public—with not only the sharing of life and faith in small groups but a whole galaxy of liturgies celebrated at various stages with the entire community. That can be a problem—for shy people, for people who have been hurt by people, for people like Lucy who says to Charlie Brown, "I love humanity. It's people I can't stand." It is also a cultural problem in America where one of our "ism's" is a religious privatism weak in social dimensions.

This calls for adaptation, certainly for the shy and scared and hurt—adaptations of patience and gentleness, of time to feel comfortable sharing faith, of expectations regarding public expressions of faith. But I assume that for them, and even more for the Lucy's and the privatists, a goal is still ecclesial conversion.

The RCIA is a response to God's presence in Jesus and *in community*. If God and his Christ are not experienced by a person in community, then let them rejoice in God's gifts apart from initiation into Church. If there is religious conversion that life is gift, however, with time that should lead to ecclesial conversion that people are gift. In fact, the RCIA assumes that most people will experience life and God as gift through their experience of people. Marriage Encounter is a similar experience of community. Father Jim Parker, pastor in Silverton, Oregon, tells of a man who told him, "Before I made a Marriage Encounter, I couldn't think anything good about God. Afterwards, I couldn't think of anything bad!" That could happen through the RCIA.

Third, the liturgical celebrations of the RCIA assume that faith is present and that the community has a role in helping a person discern faith. I do not intend to get into the chicken or egg dichotomy about whether liturgies create or express faith. Obviously, they do both. But the process of the RCIA assumes different levels of faith and conversion, with appropriate liturgies to express that gradual development.

The stickier question is the community's involvement in faith discernment. For example, at the time of Enrollment into the catechumenate, at the first threshold: "Before this step is taken, the candidates are required to be grounded in the basic fundamentals of the spiritual life and Christian teaching:... With the help of sponsors, catechists, and deacons, it is the responsibility of pastors to judge the external indications of these dispositions" (*RCIA*, n. 15, n. 16).

On the one hand, that can be an excuse for a new brand of imperialism akin to the automatic refusal of sacramental marriage or infant baptism to people who are not attending weekly Mass, with no attempt to know their personal story or to help them make the decision about what is genuine for them.

On the other hand, if the process is truly one of "spiritual direction," with ministers who are deeply sensitive both to the Lord and to people, the process can genuinely help people discern the changes, the conversions, the healing and thanksgiving within themselves. It also fulfills a responsibility to the wider community to avoid formalism and to build authentic communities of faith.

Two cautions. First, note we are speaking of faith, not virtue. The criterion is not sanctity, but the faith of a sinner who knows he/she is sinner and yet believes even more strongly in the forgiveness and gift of God.

Second, because every story is unique, what is immense faith and conversion for one person may not be for another. Father Ray Kemp, pastor of Saints Paul and Augustine in Washington, DC, tells of a catechumen who did not celebrate the Rite of Election. With the community's assistance she decided she was not ready. However, at Pentecost she told Ray, "At least I don't feel everyday like committing suicide!" For her, that was immense conversion; and the community thanked God with her and initiated her at Pentecost.

ASSUMPTIONS ABOUT GOD, CHRIST, CHURCH AND MINISTRIES

This will not be a course on Christianity 101. These will be some basic assumptions which give pastoral focus to the RCIA and which, I hope, do not create God in my image and likeness.

The context is the fundamental stance we take regarding the core issue of how God relates to the human, grace to nature, supernatural to natural, transcendence to immanence. Heresies have tipped the boat to one side or the other. Orthodoxies have kept the tension and the balance. And, of course, as Chesterton said, we all believe that "orthodoxy is 'my doxy.' "

I said that my focus is pastoral. The bottom line above, therefore, is ministries: the ministries of the RCIA. With that as focus, John Shea suggests we keep the transcendence-immanence tension. "Without immanence the transcendent God become a mere rumor, and without transcendence the immanent God dissolves into 'rocks, stars, and beetles.' "[14] Yet he also suggests the starting place cannot be the hyphen; we start from transcendence or immanence and move toward the opposite pole.

"When God is viewed as primarily *transcendent*, then Jesus is heavenly messenger and the pope and bishops are the guardians of the message who share it with the clergy and religious who finally communicate it to the laity. The result is a ministry *to* the people. . . . But when God is *intimately present* to his people and Jesus is understood in his concrete historicity and humanity and grass roots gatherings are fully church, then ministry tends to arise out of and belong to the people as a whole."[15]

These assumptions start from the pole of immanence.

1. About God

First, God is immanent, present with the gift of his love, to every person. The RCIA does not make God present where he was absent. The RCIA summons us to be present to God, to wake up if we have been absent, blind to the gift of his love. The process also summons communities to be more faithful expressions of God's presence; because individuals may find God effectively absent for them if others bury his presence in those bushel baskets. "He who sees me sees the Father" is a proclamation about every Christian, touched by the Spirit of the Risen Lord, but only if we see in those persons some hints of what could be seen in the Lord. Sacramental preparation in the RCIA, then, is not bringing God to people but helping them discern a presence that always has been. Sacramental preparation is also helping a community reveal and celebrate the Real Presence of the Father when they live in love (cf. 1 John 4).

Second, the RCIA assumes that in sacramental initiation we are primarily celebrating this mystery of God's love. The RCIA nowhere suggests we need to be absolved from an original evil.

I believe that is a serious lacuna. I have no desire to resurrect the black marks of original sin passed along by procreation. (Even Tertullian who was hardly a second century playboy, said that the semen of sexual union transmitted holiness, not sin.)[16] Yet many inquirers come with an overwhelming sense of evil, and sin, and God's absence. Contemporary reflection upon social sin, the sin of the world, and the mystery of evil deserves a hearing when we celebrate a passage through *death* to life.

It is refreshing, however, to find the first message to be the Good News of God's universal loving presence. That grounds all conversion—to turn from our evil and sin and turn to God's healing love. Pragmatically, it may resolve the anxiety both of adults and also of parents clamoring for infant baptism, because they were taught so well that baptism was necessary to remove original sin and to become a child of God. The RCIA says that catechumens *before baptism* "are joined to the Church and are part of the household of Christ" (*RCIA*, n. 18). The initiation process is a journey more deeply toward the Father, with appropriate celebrations along the way when we discern new depths of his love. The love is always there. It may take time to heal our blindness so we can plumb its depths and turn to the Lord in Baptism-Confirmation- Eucharist, believing that he has *already* turned toward us. Ministers will help us discover that "already."

Third, this conversion to the immanent, present and loving Father still leaves us hungry for more, for the transcendent God. We shall discern the presence of God in our own story and in the lives and faith of God's people. The paradox is that the more we taste of God's love in those who live in love and the more hints we have of the mystery of love, the more we become convinced that love is Mystery which surpasses all we have tested. The starting points were those tastes and hints. But the terminal point is with Augustine, "My heart is restless until it rests in Thee."[17] God is *not yet* fully present, and ministers will help people discover that "not yet."

2. About Jesus

An approach to the mystery of Jesus by way of immanence is the most frequent approach in Scripture and also in the Antiochean school in the early Church (a Christology from below). It reflects the contemporary rediscovery of the humanity of Jesus. By pondering the depths of the mystery present in him, we move toward belief in the transcendent God who is the only One who saves.

A first assumption, therefore, is that the RCIA process assumes a thoroughly robust and vigorously human Jesus, like to us in everything but sin (cf. Hebrews 4-5 and the Council of Chalcedon). He is flesh of our flesh and bone of our bone, fellow traveler on the human journey through death to life.

That is the key: Jesus as *fellow traveler*. Spiritual journey is the key theme of the RCIA. The critical question, therefore, is this: *does my personal story find meaning in the story of Jesus so that my story becomes God's story?*

I assume the answer would be a resounding "No!" if Jesus and the rest of us were on a "two-track" system, with Jesus taking the high road and us the low road. If Jesus' story is pure myth, with no roots in our history, if he never knew our human moments of crushing pain and exquisite joy, if his final question, "Why have you abandoned me?" is pure show and play acting *as if* he really knew the emptiness in the human drama, then he has very little if anything to say to the stories of others who journey in that drama.

I assume the response would be a eucharistic "Amen!" if Jesus travels with us every step of the way through death to life. If his times of temptation in the desert were "for real," if he truly felt the anguish of accepting a vocation as suffering Servant of Yahweh, if he really looked upon that rich young man with love and felt within himself the rejection of the poor and the leper and the adulterous woman and the tax collector, if he wept those real tears over Jerusalem when chicks refused his wings and over Martha and Mary when he discovers their brother decaying in death, if he drank every last drop from the human cup and still died with absolute trust that his Father would bring life from death—"Father! In your hands I place my spirit!" (Luke 23:46)—then Good News can resonate (re-sound) in our stories. Our story, too, can become God's story of what he does with us when we place our lives in his hands.

Second, the RCIA assumes that what God has done with Jesus is "raised him to the highest place above and gave him the name that is greater than any other name" (Philippians 2:10) and made him Risen Lord. Jesus is risen into the life of God, so that all the ways in which God is present in love to us are now shared by the humanity of Jesus. The assumptions about God's universal presence to every human story, his special presence in communities of faith, the celebration of his presence in the liturgy are true of the transfigured humanity of Jesus. The presence of the *risen* Christ is a key to exploring the mystery of presence in the RCIA and in all the sacraments.

Finally, the path through immanence and the humanity of Jesus once again can be the path to transcendence. From some sides we hear that religion has become too "humanistic." The problem is not humanism but a purely secular or atheistic humanism which offers a feeble and flabby view of the human. The problem is we are not sufficiently humanistic. The norm of humanity is the self-giving and risen Jesus. If we are humanistic enough, if we travel deeply enough into the human Jesus, the faith of Christians is that we shall discover the more-than-human. We discover so much healing, compassion, self-giving love and life that we come to the faith that the transcendent God must be present here. There is so much goodness, only God "could make this man." His story is possible only if it is God's story. If we go deeply enough into our own humanity, we might discover traces of the same.

3. About Church and Ministries

I mentioned earlier that the RCIA raises the most fundamental issues about Church. The way we initiate new members says what we believe Church to be. At initiation, every group wants to put its best foot forward. The question about our past practice is this: have we put our best Body of Christ forward?

"Father Smith Instructs Jackson" took a transcendent, "top-down," basically hierarchical approach to Church. It said the crux of initiation is passing on doctrine from authority. That is not wrong, and the best pastors always did more than that. But it is not the Church of Vatican II which in the *Constitution on the Church* raised the same basic issues—and came up immanent, "bottom-up," basically (with some notable exceptions) a community approach to Church.

Therefore, the first assumption about Church is that the RCIA process begins where *Lumen Gentium* begins: the Church is the Mystery of God's presence in the world through the gift of the Spirit of the risen Christ.

Before the Council met, the first draft of that document began with the hierarchy. The Council insisted on beginning with God. The RCIA process is best grounded on the same progression: the Mystery of God's presence spread broadside, giving birth to a People of God, who in turn give birth to ministries, offices, hierarchies.

That leads to a second assumption: the basic model of Church in the RCIA is Church as Community. In 1975 Bishop Albert Ottenweller presented two models of Church to the American bishops. The first is Church as *Institution* seen as professional, recognized ministers offering services (sometimes very good services) at an institutional center. He also said that Vatican II created a panoply of new programs which were to appear on the marquee at the center. For the most part they starred the same actors. The actors were already over-booked; no wonder they often never even made it for dress rehearsal.

The RCIA, in that model of Church, is a coming attraction which never came and perhaps should not come. If pastors especially see this as one more program in which Father Smith not only instructs but evangelizes, catechumenizes, illuminates, and celebrates Jackson—God help Father Smith and Jackson!

The RCIA assumes Bishop Ottenweller's second model of Church, which he described as *Community*, a People of God, all gifted by the Mystery of God's presence, perhaps helped to discern and sharpen their gifts at the institutional center, but empowered to share those gifts in small communities of faith. That is the vision of the RCIA, so much so that even catechumens minister to the wider community at various stages of their journey to the Lord by revealing what the Good News means to them.

From that vision, enter a third assumption: every member of the Church is *missionary*—on mission to share the Good News of their faith story.

I will flesh out this assumption with a detour, a footnote, and a prod.

Detour: at present there is controversy over the niceties of theological language. Is everyone on mission a "minister"? For example, Richard McBrien suggests a "ministry" in the *strict* theological sense is a service officially recognized by some form of the Church institution through appointment, installation, or ordination. At one point, he called everything else ministry in the *broad* sense. Later, he tightened his ministerial belt and suggested everything else be called apostolic witness or service.[18] I have addressed this issue more at length elsewhere.[19] It is not clear to me how broadly the RCIA is using the term "ministry." In a section entitled "Ministries and Offices" (nos. 41-48), the document begins by speaking of the responsibilities of all the faithful to surround the new Christians with their witness and their presence. Ministry seems to be used more broadly than office. For the purposes of this book, therefore, I shall be using ministries in the broad sense.

More important than terminology, the call to be missionary and to be concerned vitally about initiation of new members is issued to the entire community: "The people of God, represented by the local Church, should always understand and show that the initiation of adults is its concern and the business of all the baptized" (*RCIA*, n. 41).

The footnote: this is not an assumption, but I have found it helpful to look at the one *mission* of sharing the Good News of God's loving presence with four sets of eye-glasses which we could call *ministries*: the ministry of the Word ("kerygma"); the ministry of Community-building ("koinonia"); the ministry of Celebrating ("leiturgia"); and the ministry of Serving-healing

Figure #4

Society of Ministers	Variety and Complementarity of Ministries				
	Word	Community Building		Celebration	Serving-Healing
		Catechumenate Community	Local Community		
Those Mandated	The Catechist	The Sponsor	The Parish Council	The Ordained Ministers	Those Engaged in: •Charitable Work •Social Justice •Development
Their Collaborators	Special Catechists	Relatives and Friends	Parish Leaders	The Parents The Sponsors The Catechists	Their Assistants
The Total Community	All Christians	All the Community	All the Community	All the Liturgical Assembly	All the Community
The Local Leader	The Director of Religious Education	The Spiritual Advisor	The Pastor or Leader of The Community	The Priest	The Deacon
The Diocesan Leader	The Bishop	The Bishop	The Bishop	The Bishop	The Bishop

Note: The Director of the Rite of Christian Initiation in the community co-ordinates all the ministries.

("diakonia").[20] Figure 4 gives some sense of the relationship of these ministries to the RCIA. Indeed, they overlap. They are four ways of looking at the one Mystery of God and the one mission to share his presence. But the figure may give some way of highlighting dimensions of that mission. Note that all the particular ministries at some point get rooted in the ministry of the total community. Unless the fine talk of catechists gets grounded in a community which believes the Good News, and unless the fine care of sponsors gets validation in the wider community, there will be little to sustain on-going conversion.

That leads to the prod. Some complain that you cannot begin the RCIA until the parish or local community gets converted. There is some truth to that. Witness the religious communities which put a freeze on accepting new applicants until they got their house in order.

My sense is that we have done enough of that since Vatican II. One way to get your house in order is to stop the navel-gazing and dive into mission. One way to begin the RCIA process would be to spend a year with catechists and sponsors, a small group, who would experience the process themselves and share it with new members the following year. Then, let it spread. My experience is that people find nothing more exciting than the prospect of welcoming new members; it gives them something genuine and concrete for which to meet and learn and grow. Gradually, because the process takes place before "God and everyone," others in the community want in on the action. I believe the Lord promised something about mustard seeds growing!

ASSUMPTIONS ABOUT CATECHESIS AND LITURGY

This is not the place to get into hoary assumptions and discussions about the nature of catechesis as distinct from religious education as distinct from liturgy. For our purposes, I believe the *National Catechetical Directory* highlights in general but sufficient terms the relationship between catechesis and liturgy:

"Both are rooted in the Church's faith, and both strengthen faith and summon Christians to conversion, although they do so in different ways. In the liturgy the Church is at prayer, offering adoration, praise, and thanksgiving to God, and seeking and celebrating reconciliation: here one finds both an expression of faith and a means for deepening it. As for catechesis, it prepares people for full and active participation in liturgy (by helping them understand its nature, rituals, and symbols) and at the same time flows from liturgy, inasmuch as, reflecting upon the community's experiences of worship, it seeks to relate them to daily life and growth in faith" (*Sharing the Light of Faith*, n. 113).

Yet I offer some assumptions that I hope will indicate an even more intimate relationship between catechesis and liturgy by suggesting that "both strengthen faith and summon Christians to conversion" in some of the *same* ways. I hope these assumptions might heal the rift between catechists and some liturgists who accuse catechists of using liturgy as a "teaching device for information." More often catechesis is full of symbol and story, wonder and prayerfulness, silence and mystery, imagination and appreciation—*just as is liturgy*.

The assumptions are these: *both* the catechesis and liturgy in the RCIA process have the following priorities. They are:

More centered on:	Than on:
Conversion	Knowledge
Personal change	"Changes in the church"
Heart	Head
Growth in community	Growth in private
Journey	Arrival
Adults	Children
Faith	"The" Faith
Imagination	Logic
Right hemisphere of brain	Left hemisphere
Appreciation	Information
Mystery	Fact
Values	Laws
Gift	Problem
Immanence to transcendence	"Top down" to "'Bottom up"

37

The energetic reader may want to fill out the "why's" of all those assumptions regarding priorities. The perceptive reader may use them as a summary of all the rest of the prior assumptions. As for me, I am tired of assumptions. So I will just make one defensive remark. Note, the opposite poles are "more" and "than" not "always" and "never." Now, let us move on.

3. The Period of Precatechumenate or Inquiry

The four *periods* are: Precatechumenate, Catechumenate, the Lenten period of Illumination, the paschal period of Mystagogia. There are three *stages*, to use RCIA terminology, marking the transitions between these periods: the Rite of Becoming Catechumens, the Rite of Election or Enrollment of Names, and the Celebration of the Sacraments of Initiation. Note that catechesis and liturgy are intimately connected as we move through the catechesis of the periods (which are also marked by frequent liturgies). Each period culminates in the celebrations of the transition-stages and the veritable orgy of parties and celebrations of the period of mystagogia.

We shall journey through each period asking three questions:

1. Who are the journeyers during this period?
2. Who are the ministers?
3. What are the catechesis and liturgies?

This presumes that people will co-operate and "inquire" at the proper time, for example, and have the good taste to have "initial conversion" only *after* we have prepared them and given permission! No, the Lord is guiding the process. The following divisions are for the sake of convenience, and they may indicate when certain dimensions of the process might happen for many people.

These dimensions should happen for everyone sometime, we hope. For example, the precatechumenate is a time for sharing our personal story so it can be put in dialogue with the story of Jesus. For a shy person, perhaps that dialogue will take place within himself or herself during this period. We hope, however, that given time in an atmosphere of hospitality and trust, confidence will grow so that by the time of the period of mystagogia that same person will be able to share what has happened to him or her in some appropriate way.

THE PERIOD OF THE
PRECATECHUMENATE, OR INQUIRY[21]

1. Who are the Inquirers?

Perhaps, for this period a prior question is: Where are the inquirers? With Andrew Greeley, I am convinced they are out there, somewhere. Greeley states:

> The basic religious needs and functions have not very noticeably changed since the late Ice Age; what changes have occurred make religious questions more critical rather than less critical in the contemporary world.[22]

The difference in our age is that many people who raise serious questions do not find our churches receptive to a serious quest. During the past month I have talked with two people who said, "The last place I would share anything important about my life is the parish," and another who said, "I turned away from the Catholic Church because the priest told me my questions were a sign of pride." Perhaps the first Good News which these people want to hear is not about a Church which has all the answers, but about a hospitable, welcoming community of fellow journeyers who raise together the most important questions.

It is at this point, therefore, before the precatechumenate begins, that the parish team will want to integrate all its efforts at evangelization into the RCIA process. Without evangelization and outreach, there may be no inquirers to inquire. But without the RCIA and the vibrant community of faith and shared ministry which it envisions, outreach may summon inquirers, but there may be nothing worth inquiring about.

The United States Bishop's Committee on Evangelization offers many methods and techniques for outreach. My plea is not to neglect the power built into the RCIA process itself to proclaim Good News to inquirers. For example, people soon learn that parishes implementing the RCIA are those which take welcoming and outreach seriously. One such parish in Chicago receives calls from all over the city, "I hear this is the place where you are supposed to become a Catholic." In another parish, the newly initiated shared their faith stories during the Sunday homilies of the Paschal Season; the response was phone calls inquiring, "How can I be part of what those people have done?"

So before the precatechumenate, the parish planning team may want to try bulletin announcements, radio spots, posters and bumper stickers, and census calls. The most powerful invitation, however, to hear the Good News comes from the life of the community itself in which people can see that this parish truly lives and wants to share Good News. "See how those Christians love each other."

Now, who are the inquirers?

Dietrich Bonhoeffer in his *Letters from Prison*:

Who am I? They often tell me
I stepped from my cell's confinement
calmly, cheerfully, firmly,
like a Squire from his country house.

Who am I? They often tell me
I used to speak to my wardens
freely and friendly and clearly,
as though it were mine to command.

Who am I? They also tell me
I bore the days of misfortune
equably, smilingly, proudly,
like one accustomed to win.

Am I then really that which other men tell of?
Or am I only what I myself know of myself?
Restless and longing and sick, like a bird in a cage,

41

struggling for breath, as though hands were compressing my throat,
yearning for colors, for flowers, for the voice of birds,
thirsting for words of kindness, for neighborliness,
tossing in expectation of great events,
powerlessly trembling for friends at an infinite distance,
weary and empty at praying, at thinking, at making,
faint, and ready to say farewell to it all.

Who am I? This or the other?
Am I one person today and tomorrow another?
Am I both at once?
A hypocrite before others,
and before myself a contemptible, woebegone weakling?
Or is something within me still like a beaten army
fleeing in disorder from victory already achieved?
Who am I? They mock, these lonely questions of mine.
Whoever I am, Thou knowest, O God, I am thine! [23]

Ideally, inquirers are seekers, people on the great search for meaning. Even though they have not been in a Nazi prison like Bonhoeffer, they have experienced their own enslavements and liberations. They bring at least two things: their own stories and their questions about their stories.

John E. Smith speaks of three categories of these "ultimate questions:" The "from whence" questions: the question of the past—where have I come from; what are the key events and who are the key people who have helped make me who I am; does all of that "explain" me or has there been a Presence in my life more than all this; is there a Creator-God? The "whither" questions: the question of the future—where am I going; to what drummer's beat am I marching; what is my purpose in life; what is set before me; is the Kingdom of God set before me? The question of responsibility: if that is my past and my future, what are my responsibilities along the way? [24]

These are the kind of human-life questions which Andrew Greeley suggests are behind the great mysteries of Christianity. He translates Baltimore Catechism questions into: is there any purpose in my life? Are there any grounds for hope? Is it safe to trust? Why is there evil in the world? Is human nature totally depraved? Can our guilt be wiped away? Is it possible to have friends? Can there be unity among humankind? Can we live in harmony with nature? Can we find our sexual identity? Why is life not fair? Will we ever find peace?[25] Do Jesus and the Church say anything to these questions?

These are the kinds of questions which the precatechumenate should give people the courage and freedom to raise. My conviction is that underneath their shyness, fears and sometimes massive defenses, everyone has these questions. It may take time to surface them. The precatechumenate encourages people to "ask their very best."

In the meantime, there may be other questions. Inquirers will have very *personal questions* such as: who will meet me if I knock on that rectory door? Will anyone go up there with me? If I go to sessions to inquire about the Church, who will be there? Will I be accepted? Will I have anything to say? Do I have to say anything? How long will it take?

Inquirers will have very *Catholic* questions: why do they ring the bells at Mass? What is purgatory? Why do Catholics confess to a priest? When do you use holy water?

They may have some very *churchy* and some very hard questions for the local church: why don't these people sing at Mass? What is a parish council? Who really runs the show? Why does the St. Felicity Society exist? Why do Catholics leave Mass early?

Some will have *no questions*. Perhaps better, they will *voice* no questions. Some are shy and frightened. Others are preparing for marriage to a Catholic and thought it would be "nice" to join the same Church. Others have deep wounds and have had to face their questions alone, so they walled them off with massive defenses and now have a hard time letting them out. Others are biblical or doctrinal fundamentalists who are afraid of questions and just want answers. A priest once said to me, "What's all this search for meaning? Who cares what it means! Just believe it!"

All of this needs to be accepted. There are no "invalid nonquestions." Everyone has a personal journey which explains the level of their search for meaning on that journey.

The great challenge of the precatechumenate, however, is to help people share that journey in such an atmosphere of trust that the ultimate, human life questions begin to sneak out. Why? Because it is for these questions that Jesus and his people have Good News. So the challenge to ministers is to create that trusting environment so that people can "ask their very best." The words of Antoine de Saint-Exupery may be a bit strong, but they do encourage us "to grasp others by the shoulder while there is still time": "Old bureaucrat, my comrade, it is not you who are to blame. No one helped you to escape. You, like a termite, built your peace by blocking up with cement every chink and cranny through which the light might pierce. . . . You have chosen not to be perturbed by great problems, having trouble enough to forget your own fate as man. You are not the dweller upon an errant planet and do not ask yourself questions to which there are no answers. You are a petty bourgeois of Toulouse. Nobody grasped you by the shoulder while there was still time. Now the clay of which you were shaped has dried and hardened, and naught in you will ever awaken the sleeping musician, the poet, the astronomer that possibly inhabited you in the beginning."[26]

At least, let us awaken the person of faith.

A final note about "who are the inquirers?" Some inquirers may already be awakened in faith. Some may be nonfundamentalist Protestants with a heritage very close to the Catholic tradition who have been nourished well in their own tradition. Some may be persons who have been worshiping and learning with Catholics for many years.

The purpose of the precatechumenate is to learn about those stories of faith, not just the stories of those who are still not only searching for faith but even for the deeper questions of meaning. The precatechumenate must be flexible enough to honor all these persons; and the entire process must be so flexible that persons already strong in faith are encouraged with the help of spiritual direction to discern that they may not need a catechumenate. They might proceed directly to the third period of the RCIA which prepares them for full reception or the sacraments of initiation. If sufficient time is allowed during the RCIA process for personal interviews with each candidate (and these interviews should take place at least before the precatechumenate, before the catechumenate, before the Rite of Election, before the sacraments of initiation, and before Pentecost), the process will respect the unique character of each journey.

2. Who are the Ministers?

Perhaps for years, informally the ministers have been a spouse, a friend, a neighbor, a professional colleague, the Catholic parish next door. Ministers have been that *sponsoring community* which preceded the official ministry of sponsor in the very early Church. They have been people not necessarily "out to make others Catholic," but like Mother Teresa they have a passion to live and share the Good News of Jesus' healing love.

The RCIA presumes that throughout the formal initiation process the most important ministers continue to be this sponsoring community: "The people of God, represented by the local church, should always understand and show that the initiation of adults is its concern and the business of all the baptized" (*RCIA*, n. 41).

During the precatechumenate, for example, the document states: "Therefore they will be ready to open up the spirit of the Christian community to the candidates, to invite them into their families, to engage them in private conversation, and to invite them to some community gatherings" (*RCIA*, n. 41, 1).

Later paragraphs call for the active involvement of all the faithful in the local church at the celebrations. The document asks for their testimony concerning the growth of these new Christians, their good example and hospitality for these new members of the Church. It is here that Ralph Keifer's charge rings true: these expectations are so far removed from the pastoral practice in most parishes that this is either suicide or prophecy of the highest order.

Clearly, then, the people of the local community need to return to the origins of Church as a missionary people and a worshiping people. The extraordinary zeal of a few catechists and sponsors cannot in most cases make up for the deadweight of a parish experienced by the inquirers as inhospitable, passive observers at liturgy, and irritated and bored by "all this time and all these ceremonies" devoted to the RCIA process. Talk about old wineskins burst by new wine!

My own bias, however, is that the best way to call the local church to mission and to worship is to gradually expose and involve more and more people in the RCIA process itself. I know of no better way to give people a jolt and make them sit up and take note of what it means to be Church then to expose them to the journey in faith taken by these pilgrims who are joining the community. The beauty of the RCIA is that this journey is celebrated publicly for all to see, and (as we shall see) it involves more and more people as catechists, sponsors, special ministers. It will be difficult the first two or three years, but in time these celebrations and this growing involvement of special ministers will challenge and summon forth the ministry of the community as a whole.

The special ministers who act in the name of the entire community during this initial period in the RCIA process include the *parish director* of the RCIA plus her/his planning team. These people have reflected long and hard for many weeks before the first sessions with the inquirers in order to create the environment of hospitality and welcome which communicate Good News. Kenneth Boyack suggests practical steps which can be taken by the RCIA planning team to launch the RCIA process.[27]

Catechists will also meet with the inquirers, and the inquirers might be introduced during this period to prospective *sponsors* whose formal commitment to the inquirers might be celebrated with the entire parish at the end of this period. Rather than describe official ministries of catechist and sponsor at this point, I would prefer to name some of the qualities of ministries which best respond to the needs of the inquirers. These qualities hold true for all four periods. I shall return to specific ministries later.

For inquirers ready to share their personal journey and raise ultimate, human-life questions, ministers are people who *know their own stories* and have raised *their own questions*. They are not people who "have it all together" or who "know it all." They are persons like Jesus who have dared to take the journey, face the temptations and the questions, because they have given themselves to the hands of the Father.

For inquirers who have Christian, Catholic, and churchy questions, ministers are people who have heard the message of the key stories of *Scripture*, who have been grasped by the *great* mysteries, and have had some exposure to lesser mysteries and Catholic practices or at least know where to find a quick answer in a book. My point here is that we gave the "inquiry class" to priests because they supposedly knew everything in the books. It is enough to know the key chapters in "the books," and it is more important that the knowledge be the Hebrew understanding of knowledge— "intercourse with the message." Aidan Kavanagh asserts: "Catechists of the 'new sort' might better be old people who know how to pray, the ill who know how to suffer, and the confessor who knows what faith costs than young presbyters with new degrees in religious education."[28]

I am thinking of the catechists in the base communities in Latin America who may be "primitive" regarding religious language and information about the Catholic heritage; therefore, they come for training at catechetical centers. They are hardly primitive in faith and have the knack of centering on the great mysteries and core Gospel stories.

For inquirers who are shy, wounded, afraid or unable to tell story or ask questions, or who try end-runs with questions about the minutiae of Catholic practice, ministers will be *great listeners*. They will listen for the life which is always more profound than the words. They will be patient; but when they see a "teachable moment" when the person seems ready to stop playing deuces and discard a face-card, they will make sure that the move receives attention. That may not happen with the group; it may happen while driving home with a sponsor, for example, or with a neighbor over coffee the next day.

For these same shy and wounded inquirers, there are ministers of *hospitality*. We shall return to specific ministries when discussing the catechumenate. I do want to mention the specific ministry of hospitality with precatechumenate, because it is so important at this first period of the process.

Some people will not have even the basic gifts of knowledge and language to be catechists, or the time to be sponsors. They are known throughout the parish, however, as those who are last to leave the parish grounds after Sunday Mass is over because they have been so busy talking. They are always showing up with a cake at the time of a funeral. Their homes are places of warmth and welcome. The precatechumenate is a time for welcoming, for accepting people who are asking, "I wonder if I will be accepted." Gatherings throughout the RCIA process are ideally in homes, not rectory basements or classrooms; so this is a time to search out welcoming homes presided over by ministers of hospitality.

Once again, there are no absolutes. Pastoral judgment may indicate that someone who has felt left out might blossom through this kind of generosity. I also know of two cases in which inquirers offered their homes. In both cases, the spouse was not an active Catholic but was exposed in the home to what the Church could be. In both instances, Easter celebrations included the return of the spouse. Remember, the challenge of the RCIA is to adapt!

3. What are the Catechesis and the Liturgies?

"(The precatechumenate) is a time of evangelization: in faith and constancy the living God is proclaimed, as is Jesus Christ, whom he sent for the salvation of all men" (*RCIA*, n. 9).

My critique of the document is that evangelization, *telling* the Good News, is only half the story. The other half is *listening* to a life.

A study by Jean Haldane confirms what many people sense intuitively: that there is for a good number of people little relationship between their personal religious journey and the key events of their lives with the message and activities of the institutional Church. She says this: "I am struck by the fact that the church does seem to be concerned with *telling* and not with *listening*. Although telling is a central task of the church as it proclaims the good news, this study tells us clearly that we must pay attention to what happens to the lay people who do the listening and receiving most of the time. . . . They were dissatisfied because there was 'no place and no one' with whom to talk it over. (And they do not mean the traditional 'inquirers class'—they are not looking for 'telling' but for dialogue about meaning, in *relationship* to doctrine and their own pilgrimage.)"[29]

From the very beginning, the Church should be experienced by the inquirer as a "we" not a "they," a community of persons with stories to share not as a thing. Is it not the experience of most inquirers that they were first attracted to the Church by persons, perhaps persons with whom they had lived for many years? A recent study conducted in seven dioceses by the U.S. Bishop's Ad Hoc Committee on Evangelization confirms this. The directors of the study conclude that conversions or reconversions stem from personal relationships with committed Catholics; and books, radio and television shows alone do not do the job. One of the directors, Dean Hoge of Catholic University, says, "A conversion needs two things—a 'felt need' and a 'facilitator.'" The felt need is something like a spiritual hunger, a desire for unity in the family or a desire for the religious education of children; and the facilitator is a practicing Catholic who has a personal relationship with the person in need.[30]

Too often our catechesis failed to get those "felt needs" on the table because our catechists were tellers and lecturers, not "facilitators." We sometimes gave the impression the Church was not a "we" of fellow travelers with shared felt needs but rather those officials "back then" or "over there" who gave us this catechism to learn, these ceremonies to use, and these laws to follow. Facilitators would have set up that dialogue between the needs of inquirers and the stories of Jesus and his people.

I have already suggested that a key to the precatechumenate is the raising of questions, at various levels, but aiming at those ultimate questions of "from whence," "whither," and responsibility. The target for the questions during this period, and during the entire RCIA process for that matter, will be *stories*: a panoply of stories put into dialogue with each other.

Personal Stories. Our assumption is that God has been present during the personal religious journey of the inquirer. Catechesis will help persons raise ultimate questions about those stories so that they might personally discern God's presence (or what they may believe to be his absence). Catechists will tap the various processes available which prod us to question our lives, but not just as an exercise in "active listening" or Rogerian client-centered therapy. It is an act of faith that we are helping to unveil the presence of the Lord.[31]

Scripture Stories. There is a place for telling and evangelization and for placing personal stories in dialogue with the Big Story of Jesus and the great figures of Old and New Testament. Some claim that one of the "ism's" in our land is narcissism: the navel-gazing which gets locked into our own personal "trip." By itself, our story is without grace and is bad news. The stories of Scripture proclaim there are lives like our own to whom a God larger than life is present—and that is Good News! Remember our assumption, however: the individual is the one who decides in faith that this is Good News *for me*.

How present are the stories of Scripture during this first period? Perhaps the RCIA gives us a clue when it says that the process is reflection upon the value of the paschal mystery (*RCIA*, n. 4). Translated, that means the meaning for me of the dying and rising of Jesus. All of the stories of Scripture would be passed through this filter of dying and rising: the stories of evil in Genesis, the stories of pilgrimage and exodus to new life and faith seen in Abraham, Moses, the great prophets, the Hebrews in exile, and the key events and parables in the life of Jesus which reveal his outlandishly generous Father who offers life and Easter precisely when we think we are dead.

Admittedly, the precatechumenate is the most difficult of all the periods to structure. There are all those practical, "churchy," nuts-and-bolts questions brought by inquirers. Somewhere, those need to be addressed. Ministers also need to be sensitive to the unique journey of each of the inquirers. I am suggesting here that our Scriptures themselves are full of journey stories which have the power to unveil and deepen the meaning of each of our individual journeys. Therefore, the hallmark of this period is the dialogue between the inquirers' stories and the most moving stories of dying and rising, exodus and journey in Old and New Testament. The Good News is that God's presence and love carried Abraham, Moses, and Israel through slavery to freedom and carried Jesus through death to life. The basic inquiry of this period is: does that same Good News hold true for me?

Stories from Tradition. The great Russian author, Nicholas Berdaeyev, says that traditions are the dead faith of living people (those who say, "It's always been done that way") and Tradition is the living faith of dead people. I would add Tradition is also the living faith of living people. Tradition is the handing along and the re-living in dramatic new ways the experience of Jesus that the Father brings life out of death.

I suggest that the period of *catechumenate* is the time to ponder in depth on *past Tradition*, the living faith of dead people. To help the inquirer decide whether or not to join a Church of fellow travelers, the *precatechumenate* might expose inquirers to *living people* and their experiences of dying and rising. This would include catechists and sponsors in formal sessions, but also in informal visits and sessions the old people who know how to pray, the sick who know how to suffer, single people who have dealt with loneliness, married people who have experienced the Father's love. The question continues to be, "Do the stories of these fellow travelers bring meaning to my experiences of death and life, so much so that I want to join their company?"

A special band of companions might be the neophytes who have just completed initiation. For at least some of the sessions, inquirers might join the newly initiated during the paschal season to listen to them rejoice in what the Lord has done and is doing for them.

Parish Stories. Individuals in the parish can unfold what faith means to them personally. There is also the story, in past and present, of that parish as institution and community. Inquirers need to make a decision in the context of this *local* church.

51

Grand theories about universal Church and what the Church *should* be will forever be tested against, "See how *these* Christians love one another" or fail to love.

Part of that process will be the telling of the history of the parish, perhaps through the older people who "were there." Ray Kemp, pastor of Sts. Paul and Augustine in Washington, DC, suggests another process which gets at parish life in the present. He calls it the "hot seat." Leaders of various parish organizations come before the inquirers to tell what they offer, why they exist, and (we hope) what their existence has to do with the gospel.

Another ingredient, which broadens inquirers' perspective beyond just one parish, would be exposure to other parishes. During summer months when people might be traveling, they could be encouraged to "check out" parishes along the way and report back what they find. That may include some "horror stories," but it might begin to unveil both the foibles and strengths of the Church universal.

Two footnotes. First, a secondary goal of the precatechumenate is to give people some religious language to use in order to interpret their lives. The problem in talking about our lives is not just one of trust. Some people just do not know "how to say it." Scripture stories will give them some language about dying and rising, slavery and freedom, exile and Promised Land, exodus and journey and desert and mountain which might help them name the demons and the angels in their own pilgrimage.

Second, the precatechumenate will set the stage for a more in-depth exploration of doctrine by grounding doctrine in stories. The best catechists always have done that, but sometimes the inquiry class of the past simply presented doctrines as arid abstractions and not as capsule summaries of meaning which people in a living Tradition created when they put the journey of Jesus into dialogue with their own journey and times.

At the end of this period, inquirers will be making a decision whether or not to become a *Catholic* Christian. They often will have questions about particularly Catholic doctrines, e.g., the place of the pope in the Church. My assumption is that during this period stories about the pope are more important than the doctrine of Vatican I. The overwhelming response to Pope John Paul seems to be at that level. In fact, stories of his life give his doctrinal and ethical statements about poverty, for example, some credibility. If questions remain about papal doctrine and statements, however, I sense they could be pursued for most people during the catechumenate.

Liturgies. To make detailed suggestions about liturgies for this period or for later periods is beyond the scope of this book.[32] For the precatechumenate, the RCIA has no formal rites. However, following our previous assumptions about the relationship of catechesis and liturgy, the catechesis suggested above for this period is grounded on story, myth, symbols and images which leads easily into the world of liturgy.

The RCIA does recommend an optional ceremony of reception for inquirers at the beginning of the period and also times of prayer throughout the precatechumenate (RCIA, nos. 12-13). If an inquirer decides not to enter the catechumenate, and if he/she decides to continue exploring as an inquirer, that decision might be celebrated in prayer. All of this is left to the creativity of the ministers.

Decision. "From evangelization, conducted with the help of God, come faith and initial conversion, by which each one feels himself called away from sin and drawn toward the mystery of God's love" (RCIA, n. 10).

At the end of the precatechumenate, the decision will be whether the Catholic Christian community offers to the person journeyers who share in the healing of sin and the mystery of God's love.

The "catechesis" at this time will be discernment: helping the inquirer ask the questions which disclose the desire to die to sin and live in God's healing love. There are also questions which disclose if this best happens for her/him in the Catholic Church, because at this point as catechumens they enter membership in the Church (RCIA, n. 18).[33]

The minister might be the catechist, a spiritual director, perhaps a priest.

The place will be in a private interview, in an atmosphere of total freedom. Perhaps an interviewer who has not been intimately involved in precatechumenate sessions would help foster that freedom.

The celebration of this decision will be in the Rite of Becoming Catechumens which rejoices in the faith that personal stories are part of God's story and the stories of his people.

4. The Period of the Catechumenate

The inquirer searched and explored from outside the community. The catechumen explores from within. The RCIA calls this "initial conversion." There are the beginnings of the radical turning to life as gift, God as personal, Jesus as living, and the Church as "we." Those beginnings have moved the person to join his/her story to the stories of Jesus and his followers in the Catholic community to explore from inside that community deeper levels of conversion.

Therefore, at the heart of the catechumenate period is *conversion in community*. The person has decided that in spite of all of its sins and fumblings and bumblings the community which gathers round Jesus in faith is the place of the Lord's presence where he leads all of us on the journey to his Father. The community has become what Colman McCarthy calls "inner companions." "To have companions of any kind—inner or outer—suggests a journey is being made, as indeed with all of us there is. It should be a traveling toward gentleness, integrity and joyfulness, a destination all of us long for but hesitate to imagine ourselves reaching, lest on arrival we be given new obligations to love. But if we can travel with a band of inner companions, what tests can prove too demanding? It is not that the chosen companions of our interior, at least not the ones whom I have taken into my life, are meant to teach us matters of power and might—how to earn a living, how to make sense or make progress. Those are the most handily mastered of life's chores.

Instead, we need them to share with us the wisdom of the obvious, to repeat and repeat for our stubborn minds what we never quite get right—that all of us are fragile, that the wealth of the planet should be shared justly, and that nothing matters unless it is done with a perpetual fidelity to love."[34]

The catechumenate is an exploration in some depth of the wisdom and the living Tradition of those inner companions, especially Jesus.

1. Who are the Catechumens?

From one perspective, catechumens are still *searchers*, with the same kinds of questions that we saw in the inquirers. We hope that the atmosphere of trust and hospitality of the pre-catechumenate has moved those questions toward greater depth. A critical difference is that inquirers ask those questions as observers, from outside the community; catechumens ask them from within as fellow travelers.

A second perspective from which to view catechumens is that of their *baptismal status and their previous history* with any Christian Church. Of course, this is also true of inquirers; but that perspective raises more issues and questions during the catechumenate.

Catechumens, strictly speaking, will be unbaptized adults who have celebrated the Rite of Becoming Catechumens. (The RCIA also has a special section on initiation of unbaptized children who have reached the age of reason, nos. 306-313.) But "catechumens" will also be baptized Catholics who are uncatechized and have not completed initiation in Confirmation and Eucharist (once again, the RCIA has a special section for these people, nos. 295-305, and notes, "For the same reason as for catechumens, the preparation of these adults requires a long time," n. 296). There will be baptized Protestants with little or with strong participation in a Christian community. There may be non-Christians who have weak or rich experience in another religious tradition. How do we welcome all these people sensitively?

On the one hand, there is no question: "the sacrament of baptism may not be repeated, and conditional baptism is not permitted unless there is a reasonable doubt about the fact or validity of the baptism already received" (*RCIA Appendix*, n. 7). There is a Rite of Reception of Baptized Christians into Full Communion with the Catholic Church and "any confusion between catechumens and candidates for reception into communion should be absolutely avoided" (*Appendix*, n. 5). We take for granted an ecumenical sensitivity.

On the other hand, I believe a hint from Ralph Keifer is right on the mark: "In these years of discovering the catechumenate, we will be learning that often the great distinction in those who wish to belong in our church is not that of baptized and non-baptized, but between those who have some practice in faith (whether they are baptized or not) and those who have none (whether baptized or not)."[35]

Some unbaptized catechumens may have been involved in Catholic practice for years, e.g., participation at Sunday Eucharist. They may also be strong in faith. Some baptized Catholics or Protestants may never have entered a church door.

Pastorally, this all comes to a head over the issue of the dismissal of candidates for initiation which begins during the catechumenate and continues until their full initiation at Easter.

"Ordinarily, however, when they are present in the assembly of the faithful, they should be dismissed in a friendly manner before the eucharistic celebration begins, unless there are difficulties" (*RCIA*, n. 19:3).

When I first read the RCIA, I decided that of all the archaisms in the document, this one topped the list. After experiencing this dismissal rite in several parishes, I now say—do it! But do it for these reasons:

First, we are not "kicking them out." This is not a matter of exclusion. Sponsors and catechists leave with them after the Service of the Word to break open that Word and put it into dialogue with our personal journeys. It is a time to strengthen belief in Christ's Real Presence in his Word.

Second, it is bad catechesis and liturgy to invite catechumens to remain for a eucharistic meal which they cannot share. By osmosis this sends a message that they can refuse the Lord's invitation to "Take and eat and drink." Indeed, they may have come often to Mass without coming to Communion; or they may have been coming to Communion indiscrimately. That raises pastoral problems, but those problems should be raised as separate issues which a parish needs to resolve apart from the issue of the dismissal of catechumens.

Third, the dismissal gives powerful witness to the rest of the community concerning the depth of the journey into faith which leads to the sharing of the eucharistic meal on that journey. Sacraments are celebrations of faith, and catechumens give public witness to the challenges to grow in faith.

Fourth, there is a long, but presently neglected, practice of eucharistic fast to build anticipation of the Eucharist. For catechumens, this fast and dismissal from the communion-meal can help the Easter Eucharist become the climax of initiation.

Fifth, the decision should be that of the catechumen, as much as possible. A sensitive catechist will go over the reasons suggested above with the catechumens. If they believe these reasons are invalid for them, that decision should be honored. Most find the breaking open of the Word so helpful and their witness to the rest of the community so valuable that they do choose to leave.

Pastoral sensitivity brings us back to the question of the baptized, whether Catholic or Protestant. Should they be dismissed? Aidan Kavanagh suggests: "They should best be treated as catechumens in all things except that they are not dismissed from the Eucharist with their unbaptized colleagues; but neither should they be communicated because their baptism has not yet been publicly confirmed with the seal of the Spirit, an act in which full communion in the Spirit-filled Church comes to ecclesial and sacramental consummation."[36]

Ray Kemp suggests we explore the possibility of communicating baptized adults during the catechumenate just as we do children who have been baptized as Catholic at infancy but have not been fully initiated with Confirmation.[37]

My own sense is that the norm should be dismissal for all those in the catechumenal community, baptized or not. Kavanagh's criterion of baptism certainly honors the sacrament and other churches, but it seems to strike a bit of formalism and ritualism. Many who have been baptized may be very weak in faith.

Even for those stronger in faith, I suggest the norm would still be dismissal. It says that faith can always grow. It also says that the eucharistic meal is not the only way to experience the Lord's presence. This may be a special time to experience his presence in Word.

For those who have strong feelings about staying for the eucharistic meal, two negative possibilities follow: not eating at a meal, or communicating without the full initiation of Confirmation. Because I am so convinced it is time to move pastorally on the restoration of Baptism-Confirmation-Eucharist as the normal and integral Rite of Initiation (more of that later!), I would counsel the first alternative.

Even more difficult than the perspective of different histories regarding baptism and faith-practice is a third perspective from which to view catechumens: *levels of faith-development*. In this regard, the tentative but provoking research of James Fowler might be of assistance.[38] Who are the catechumens in terms of faith-development?

I cannot digress far into developmental research, but one insight might be encouraging. Lawrence Kohlberg in terms of moral development says that people cannot hear language which is two stages above their own level of development, but they like to hear language which challenges them from one stage beyond where they are. If that is also true of faith-language, it is not necessarily bad to have a mix of people in a catechumenal community.

Most catechumens will be literalists and fundamentalists, both regarding Scripture and doctrinal statements. It is good to have them challenged by people who have experienced intellectual conversion (from fact to meaning), and it is good to have them force others to find words to express what the data of Scripture and doctrine mean to them. In other words, it is a more genuine experience of Church in which there have always been great battles about meaning and in which there have been inarticulate, faith-filled people who challenge articulate Ph.D.'s when their words are a cover-up for faith, and articulate, faith-filled people who can help the less articulate find words to express their experience of the Lord. In brief, let us keep it "catholic"!

Exceptions to this might be non-fundamentalist Protestants who seek entry into the Catholic Church and are coming from a rich Protestant tradition which has nourished them in a faith and sacramental experience much like that of the Catholic tradition, e.g., Lutheran or Episcopalian. If this is discerned during the precatechumenate, perhaps they would choose not to become catechumens. With the help of a spiritual director, they may decide that they do not need a catechumenate but are ready to enter the immediate preparation for full reception into the Catholic Church which is offered during Lent. They would celebrate full reception at Easter, and it would be ecumenically sensitive at that time to have them and the entire community explicitly thank God for the care and nourishment they received in their Protestant tradition.

It is also conceivable that an unbaptized person who has participated in the Catholic Church for several years might be strong in faith. That person might also simply enter the Lenten period without a catechumenate and celebrate full initiation at Easter.

On the other hand, such persons who are rich in faith might choose to enter the catechumenate. They might see this as an opportunity both to deepen their faith and also to share their faith with others. Perhaps they have come seeking just such a catechumenal experience. This is a bit different than just updating Catholics, since they are entering a different Christian tradition. They might well be welcomed into the catechumenate.

A fourth pespective from which to view catechumens is from the vantage point of *cultural differences*. I wish to suggest just two imperatives. In terms of language and symbol, let there be reverence for the symbols of a given culture. In terms of the need for various types of conversion, let there be respect for the history both of individuals and of peoples.

First, let us honor the culture. Virgil Elizondo of the Mexican-American Cultural Center says: "Ten years ago we were saying comfortably that 85% of the Hispanics in the U.S. were Catholics. Today, we can at best say that 75% of them are Catholics. The Hispanic is not leaving the Catholic Church freely, he/she is still being chased out by pastors and parishes who do not want them around. . . . In the case of the Hispanic, it is often the Protestants who are providing the personal catechumenate programs while the Catholic church is still chasing them out by refusing to pray, sing, teach and celebrate in the culture and language of the people. In many instances, the U.S. Catholic Church is still insisting more on conversion from the Hispanic culture into the U.S. Anglo-Saxon-Protestant-based culture than in conversion to Christ within the Hispanic culture itself."[39]

The paradox is: without overly romanticizing "black soul" or Hispanic mariachi, at their best they may be much more open to the world of symbol, the non-rational and non-analytical, the communal world of story and myth and feeling and mystery than is the white, middle-class, mechanized and privitized culture which sets the rules for catechizing and celebrating. Our assumptions about catechesis in the RCIA are on the side of "soul" and mariachi.

Second, let us honor the history of that culture. Individual histories differ because of culture. A young adult in white suburbia and a Hispanic in a barrio may both need ecclesial conversion—but for very different reasons. The young Anglo may resent the Church institution because both parents and pastors forced religion on her at church, sometimes because there was very little religion at home. The young Hispanic, often strong in "home-religion," may resent the Church institution, because his home was not welcome there. If both become catechumens, healing will probably take very different forms.

People also have a history as a people. It was a joy to hear recently, for example, from a missionary in Africa that the church is appealing because it means liberation—from strict

tribal laws, from sexism, from oppressive governments. Catechumens with a minority history in this country will need to
experience that kind of Church and in a different way from, let
us say, the catechumen from the culture in the majority whose
history is more in need of liberation from consumerism, up-
ward mobility, competition, and mid-career crises. Many catechumens have shoddy self-images. At least the whites usually
do not need to hear "white is beautiful," but the image of mi-
norities is very much tied to a history of mutilation of brown
and black and red and yellow.

2. Who are the Ministers?

The qualities of ministers described in the previous section
obviously hold true for the catechumenate. The ministry of the
total community holds true, of course, for the entire process.
Likewise, exposure to individuals within that community—rela-
tives and friends, single and married, the suffering and the ac-
tivists, old and young, parish leadership—continues more in
depth during the catechumenate.

At this point, I want to spotlight two specialized ministries
which have special prominence during the catechumenate: the
ministry of catechist and the ministry of sponsor.

The Ministry of Catechist. I am not going to dwell at length
on the qualities of the catechist. I shall simply repeat that all
the assumptions in the early pages of this book, summed up
in assumptions about catechesis, bear special import for catechists.

In workshops around the United States, Christiane Brusselmans has offered characteristics of the catechumenate community. These summarize in a special way the qualities of
catechists:

1. A community of hospitality, friendship, and communion;
2. A community in a process of ongoing conversion;
3. A community in search of meaning;

4. A community that is attentive to God's Word—shared and interpreted with honesty;
5. A community that celebrates and worships in praise and thanksgiving;
6. A community that witnesses in the world and shares in the pastoral, prophetic, and priestly ministry of the Church;
7. A community where all members are partners in ministry.

I do want to stress that what the CCD did many years ago for the catechesis of children the RCIA does for the catechesis of adults—extend the ministry of catechist to a wide variety of people. For the catechumenate, the RCIA speaks of "a fitting formation by priests, deacons, or catechists and other lay persons, given in stages and presented integrally, accommodated to the liturgical year and enriched by celebrations of the word" (*RCIA*, n. 19:1).

Note that there is no "lay trusteeism" which ousts the priests as clericalism once gave the exit to lay people. Indeed, in missionary lands the catechists are often exclusively lay people due to a shortage of priests; and priests (who we hope are also good catechists) minister largely to the formation of lay catechists. In this country, priests who are gifted as catechists should continue to catechize.

But even where there is no shortage of priests, the complex needs of lay persons to share Tradition, faith, and their personal journey with other lay people demand a variety of catechists.

"The reinstitution of the catechumenate ... must inevitably elicit a larger and more diversified corps of catechists than we have been accustomed to in the past. What must be done for catechumens is so multiform and extensive that no one person, no matter how well trained, can accomplish it all."[40]

The Ministry of Sponsor. In the very early Church, there was no specialized ministry of sponsor but rather a sponsoring community conscious of its missionary call to invite others to meet the Lord.

Michel Dujarier asserts that the specialized ministry of sponsor which developed during the heyday of the early catechumenate and which has been restored in the RCIA has two principal roles: witness and guide.[41] These are summed up this way:

"Helped by the example and support of sponsors and godparents and the whole community of the faithful, the catechumens will learn to pray to God more easily, to witness to the faith, to be constant in the expectation of Christ in all things, to follow supernatural inspiration in their deeds, and to exercise charity toward neighbors to the point of self-renunciation" (*RCIA*, n. 19:2). If all of that is seen in sponsors, they are mighty powerful witnesses and guides and a far cry from the nod we give to sponsorship in most infant baptisms.

Dujarier suggests two dimensions to being *witness: witness to* the catechumen of what it means to be possessed by the Lord in faith, and *witness for* the catechumen before the community, especially at times of discernment at the Rite of Becoming Catechumens and the Rite of Election.

In both dimensions of witnessing, the sponsor is probably closer to the catechumen than any other minister. The sponsor attends formal sessions in the precatechumenate and catechumenate. The more important moments, however, are those informal times in conversation on the way home, or in prayer together, or in journeying through times of dying and rising together when in communion they experience the Lord. In those times, the sponsor witnesses to what the Lord means to her/him. In those times, the sponsor helps the catechumen discern what the Lord is doing in his/her life, assists the catechumen to make decisions about membership in the community, and gives public witness to the community in the liturgical rites about what the Lord is doing in the life of the new Christian.

As *guide*, the sponsor helps the person enter into the life, the customs, the ongoing ministries and celebrations of the community. Perhaps more than the catechists, the sponsor can answer the concrete questions about Church practice, especially about prayer, liturgy, the institutions and structures of the Church. The role of guide also presupposes a pre-baptismal and post-baptismal ministry: to introduce the person to the community before baptism and to stay with the person after baptism so that the person is integrated into the life of the parish.

There is some confusion in the RCIA because it speaks of both sponsor and godparent (*RCIA*, nos. 42, 43). It seems to associate sponsor with a pre-baptismal role and godparent with a post-baptismal role. The sponsor is described as a friend of the candidate, and might not be the godparent who is delegated by the community.

The concern is pastoral. Often a candidate has a good friend who is Catholic who helps the candidate make the first approach toward Church membership. But the community also has a concern that the ministries of witnessing and guidance, as described above, be offered to both candidate and to the parish. That person especially should be aware of the directions the Church is taking since Vatican II. If the "good friend" cannot do that, the community should offer someone who can. Both continue the journey with the candidate, one as friend, one as friend and witness and guide. They can flip coins over the titles of sponsor or godparent!

Two final notes: we have taken for granted that catechists deserve formation. It should be clear from the above the sponsors who act in the name of the parish deserve formation. They will receive that in part through the catechetical sessions. More important, they deserve spiritual direction to help them see more clearly in their personal journey the Lord whom they hope to witness to others.[42] After such formation, they can be publicly commissioned to represent the parish in the ministry of sponsor.

Finally, it should be clear from the description of the role of sponsors that they cannot take on too many candidates. There should be no parish "pool" of sponsors, re-cycled each year. The ministry of sponsorship should be extended to others in the parish, even if there are only one or two catechumens who need witness and guidance.

3. What are the Liturgies and the Catechesis?

Liturgies. It is time to make a point. Remember, the RCIA is a *rite*, a liturgical rite. The process is not a series of classes or instructions with a few ceremonies thrown in or perhaps tolerated because they are perceived as archaic (for too many, exorcism evokes images only of nasty little girls vomiting in *The Exorcist* or little red devils!). The whole process is aimed at worship, eucharist, thanksgiving. Every bit of the catechesis should be prayerful and lead into liturgical prayer. And for once, sacramental preparation does not lead simply to one big blast. With the RCIA there is a galaxy of lesser blasts to let off steam, to express our growing experience of the Lord's presence on the journey. Charles Gusmer pleads: "The most important thing I would urge is not to diminish or tame the catechumenal liturgies, rather take advantage of them and celebrate them to the fullest extent possible. They are not a collection of ceremonies to be dutifully executed, they are important celebrations of transitions or threshold experiences as the candidate is progressively incorporated into the Church."[43]

Liturgies during the catechumenate begin with the Rite of Becoming Catechumens which launches catechumens into a catechumenal community. This is not the place for detailed suggestions—just two points.

First, the importance of the time, for the catechumen and the parish. With all the contemporary stress on the big blast of baptism, we have forgotten our early tradition that entrance into the catechumenate was seen as entrance into the Church. Michel Dujarier identifies the images used in early catechesis to unfold its meaning. Origen saw it as entrance into the Red Sea (baptism was crossing the River Jordan into the Promised Land after the exodus of the catechumenate). In the fourth century, it was seen as conception (baptism seen as birth). It was the planting of a seed (with baptism, the seed bears fruit). It was like the acceptance by the apostles of Christ's call (which after three years culminated in their baptism through his death-resurrection). With the imagery of the

Canticle of Canticles, entrance into the catechumenate was like engagement to the beloved (which prepared for the baptismal wedding).[44] For both catechumen and parish, this is the time of heartfelt acceptance of each other: to begin the march through exodus, to grow together toward birth, to nourish the seed which will bear fruit, to spend time following the Lord on the way to Easter, and to be engaged to the Lord like those wise virgins who kept their candles burning and were ready for the wedding.

Second, adapt the rite. The rite asks for that. It provides a solid framework, but like all the rites of the RCIA it needs to leap from the stilted language of the page into personal expressions of faith from the catechumens and personal acceptance by God and his people. The symbols are powerful, e.g., the cross and signing. When Pope John Paul II celebrated this rite with catechumens in Chicago, his fussy master of ceremonies made sure he did not touch the catechumens. Symbols were emasculated. Imagine the immense possibilities for covering the person with possession by Jesus and his cross, by priest, sponsors, community.

In this rite, as in others, at times even the framework is not so solid. For example, the signing of the senses precedes the liturgy of the Word. The traditional and psychologically sound approach is to have word precede action. *If* liturgical planners know both the tradition and psychology, they should feel free to adapt.[45]

Note, an optional rite during this period is the *anointing with the oil of catechumens*. Oil and signing with the cross might be combined at this time.

Celebrations of the Word. We already noted that the norm during the catechumenate is dismissal at each Sunday Eucharist to ponder the Word of God. This assures the whole process keeps in touch with the liturgical year. Of course, this is in addition to weekly catechetical sessions, which also might include celebrations of the Word.

Minor Exorcisms. The rite provides that these be celebrated by priest, deacon, or a catechist delegated by the bishop.

"These take place in the church, the sacristy, or the catechumenate center, during a celebration of the word. They may also be held at the beginning or end of the gathering for instructions; on account of special needs, they may be done privately for individual catechumens" (*RCIA*, n. 110).

Many catechumens come with an immense sense of evil and guilt and with great needs for healing. Our tradition says that evil (which is more than little red devils) is cast out by prayer and fasting and almsgiving, not so much by instructions. If we are sensitive to all the demons in our culture and our personal lives, this will open countless opportunities for prayer and exorcism.[46]

Presentations of the Creed and the Lord's Prayer. These rites can be celebrated during the third period, Illumination; but especially if the catechumenate is extended to twelve months or longer, they might appropriately "beef up" the catechumenate.

The Presentation of the Creed can recall the dry, rote monotone recitations of some catechism classes; or it can be a personal surrender to Persons who summon our faith, not just to articles of faith. The celebrant can proclaim our belief first in Father, then Jesus, Spirit, and Church, and invite catechumens and sponsors and the entire assembly to express what these persons mean to them.

The Presentation of the Lord's Prayer need not be a strange ritual giving us what we already know; it can be a similar summons to personally enter the Lord's *way of praying*. Jesus offers a model for all prayer: praise of the Father, and then voicing our need for blessing and healing. The celebration might invite all present to do just that.

In both cases, the emphasis is on handing over a living Tradition of personal faith in persons and a way of praying.

Footnote: in all these rites, spontaneity and personal expressions of faith will be difficult. If this happens first in small gatherings, it may be easier with the parish community. For those who can never "tell it like it is" out loud in public, at least times of silence allow them to voice it in their hearts so that rite becomes not dry rite (or dry rot!) but worship in spirit and truth.

Catechesis. The formation recommended by the RCIA has four dimensions: 1) personal integration of the great biblical and doctrinal themes of Christianity; 2) assistance in living the Christian way of life; 3) liturgical celebrations; 4) apostolic sharing of the Gospel with others (*RCIA*, n. 19). Comments follow on 1) in terms of themes for catechesis, and 4) in terms of discerning a service or ministry.

Themes for Catechesis. First, a defensive remark; then a few suggestions not for detailed catechesis but for general approaches.

First, I suggested that catechesis in the RCIA was more concerned with heart than head, imagination than logic, appreciation than information. That could be heard as a mindless call to reject thinking and intelligence in the name of private revelations from the Spirit, infallible feelings with little room for even fallible thinking, and "show and tell" sessions or "group-gropes" in which we create the Word of God in our image and likeness because we are all "born again" with an infallibility far more oppressive than the pope's could be.

In defense, let me affirm, especially during the catechumenate, the need for some critical, analytical, patient, yet wonder-filled thinking which proceeds not only from guts but from cortex. For catechists, that especially means some study of contemporary research in Scripture, and some exposure to the history of doctrinal development and systematic theology.

Both types of study will be liberating. Scripture studies ultimately will free us to discern meaning and not just the literal readings of fundamentalists or the purely personal interpretations forced on Scripture by some who are "born again." Historical and theological studies will also free us to discern meaning for lives in our times and in our language; because we discover that is precisely what our Latin and Greek and European forbears did for their lives, times, and language. Sometimes people will have some hard questions about Real Presence, about infallibility, about issues in sexual ethics. They deserve more than our gut reactions.

I shall suggest three general approaches for catechumenal catechesis which a team of us have been offering throughout the country in workshops: 1) through the history of salvation; 2) through the names and titles of Jesus; 3) through ultimate questions.

Certainly most consonant with the RCIA and with the formation of most catechists would be the approach through the *history of salvation*. The approach is primarily biblical, with a constant dialogue between Bible stories and our stories. It also moves beyond Bible through the continuing history of salvation in the living Church until our own times.

Christiane Brusselmans suggests taking the *names of Jesus* and then moving backwards to Israel and forward towards ourselves. We begin with Jesus as Suffering Servant, move back to Israel as the suffering Servant of Yahweh, and forward to the healing God who calls us to servanthood. We begin with Jesus as Word, then listen to his Word in all those prophets before him, and listen for his Word in all the ways it speaks to us today.

A third approach begins with *ultimate questions*, which is really the approach of the Baltimore Catechism although for many of us its questions did not seem ultimate. This approach would use the inquiry period to set the stage for the catechumenate by identifying the questions of personal importance for which we hope to find meaning in the living Tradition of Jesus and his people. This would be the approach suggested by Andrew Greeley in *The Great Mysteries*.[47]

I leave it to the reader to find materials which enflesh these approaches. If any of these approaches have touched our own personal journey, that is the critical issue. I have a hunch we shall find the books which help express what the Lord has already said to us in silence.

The basic text, of course, is the Bible. Bibles could be presented as gifts to the catechumens during the welcoming rite.

Note: although the entire RCIA process is an exploration of the real presence of the Lord in our spiritual journeys, reflection upon Real Presence in sacraments for the most part should take place during the period of mystagogia. The mystagogical principle of the Fathers was this: you cannot understand what you have not experienced. We cannot tell people what sacramental symbols will mean to them. The symbols first have to grasp them with all of their power, and then the person can reflect upon what she/he has experienced. Certainly, the experience of the Lord in human moments will easily lead into sacramental moments in liturgy, but sacramental catechesis should happen after sacramental celebration.

Apostolic Witness. Just a brief note, because we shall come back to this in the period of mystagogia. That is the time to reflect upon our experience of the mysteries of dying and rising in the sacraments, and that is also the time when the new Christian determines how to extend those mysteries of dying and rising by offering his/her gifts in service or ministry.

That process needs some data for discernment, however. Therefore, from the very beginning, when the person enters the Church as a catechumen, there should be exposure to what other Catholic Christians are doing to proclaim the Good News. That applies especially to the area of social justice. Since the RCIA process can be deeply personal experience of the Lord, perhaps for the first time, broader issues of the community and justice might be neglected. That is understandable, but the catechesis constantly needs to relate personal conversions to God with God's concern for the hungry, thirsty, naked, prisoner, and the poor. The catechumenate will help catechumens discern their gifts and share them. That means they also get the Sunday envelopes!

I shall close this section on the catechumenate with a concession. Thus far, I have resisted offering time-lines or calendars for the RCIA. I hope you are convinced by now that the journeys of unique persons to the Lord cannot be programmed. For example, some inquirers, as we have noted, may not need a catechumenate; others might spend two or three years in a catechumenate.

However, I am aware that 95% of the parishes which have implemented the RCIA have adopted a 9-month time-line; generally, precatechumenate runs September through November; catechumenate begins on the First Sunday of Advent; enlightenment on the First Sunday of Lent; with mystagogia during the Easter season.

I believe this does not give many people enough time before the Rite of Becoming Catechumens and before the Rite of Election to get some distance from the process and ponder seriously these times of transition. I also believe the time is too short to enter deeply into the Catholic Tradition. That is not a matter simply of getting time to "get all the doctrine in." It is more a matter of attitudes and values, Gospel values which are in tension and conflict with so many demons and principalities and powers of American culture. Those same tensions and conflicts with culture convinced Christians in the early centuries that the catechumenate demanded time.

If parishes determine that their first efforts at the RCIA have to be within a nine-month time-line, that is understandable. As Bishop John Cummins of Oakland has said, "If it's worth doing, it's worth doing badly!" I believe he is saying that it is more important to try the RCIA and perhaps make a few mistakes the first time.

However, I would like to suggest another calendar for those who are uneasy with conversion in nine months. This calendar was developed by Father John Costanzo and the staff at Sacred Heart Parish in Alamosa, Colorado; and I believe it gives more time for discernment and more time to be integrated into a true community of faith and values.

> **Precatechumenate:** Informal meetings with the newly initiated after Easter to hear their conversion stories; social gatherings with parishioners during the summer months; introduction to parish leaders; personal interviews. Formal sessions September through November.
>
> **Decision Time:** December

Catechumenate: January of one year to January of the next year; sessions four times each month, with one session a month in the summer.

Decision Time: January

Illumination: First Sunday of Lent until Holy Week

Mystagogia: Easter until Pentecost

Note that in this model a new group would begin each September with formal sessions in the precatechumenate; one group would begin before the first group had concluded. Also in this parish sponsors meet with inquirers who come too late to be included in a catechumenal community. The sponsors keep contact and deal with the inquirer's needs and questions until a new group begins formal meetings in September.

5. The Period of Illumination

In November, 1654, Blaise Pascal heard a sermon in which the preacher proclaimed the demand for entire surrender to God. He fell into a trance shortly after this, and had a vivid impression of the presence of God. The record of this experience was found after his death on a paper worn over his heart:

> The year of grace 1654, Monday, November 23rd. . . from about half past ten in the evening to about half past midnight. Fire.
>
> God of Abraham, God of Isaac, God of Jacob. Not of the philosophers and of the learned. Certainty. Certainty. Feeling. Joy. Peace. God of Jesus Christ. "Deum meum et Deum vestrum." Thy God shall be my God—Forgetful of the world and of all except God. One finds him only by the ways taught in the Gospel. Greatness of the human soul. Righteous Father, the world has not known thee, but I have known thee. Joy, joy, joy, tears of joy . . . My God will you leave me? May I not be separated from him eternally.
>
> This is eternal life, knowing thee the only true God and the one sent by you J.-C. Jesus Christ. I have been separated from him: I have fled from him, renounced him, crucified him. May I never be separated from him.[48]

The joy of ministering during this third period of purification, enlightenment, and illumination is sharing stories of such moments of grace, in language more of the 20th century but full of the same Fire, Joy, and Peace.

This period coincides with Lent and resounds with the message that Lent is thrust toward baptism. The energies, prayer, penance, fasting, the vision and concern of the entire parish are mobilized to surround these new Christians as they journey toward the climax of their pilgrimage. Lent without candidates for baptism is like a Mass without bread and wine. These persons are the sacraments of the dying and rising taking place in all of us. They are the symbols to be transformed who also transform us.

The period is launched by the Rite of Election, the crossing of the second threshold at the end of the catechumenate by those ready to celebrate the Father's election of them into his people. It concludes with the sacraments of initiation at the Easter Vigil.

1. Who are the Elect?

This is a difficult word and an even more difficult judgment for egalitarian Americans raised on a democratic diet in which "all are created equal." Election smacks of favoritism. It gets even more complicated when we learn that the community has some say in who gets elected for baptism.

On the one hand, then, on the side of Good News, mercy, healing, the outlandish love of the Father, and the principle that everything in Judaeo-Christianity begins with God's initiative, the message is—God chooses everyone. Our God scurries around looking for lost sheep and coins, summons pint-sized tax collectors out of trees, overpays latecomers in vineyards, and comes running down the road with embraces and rings and robes and shoes and prize calves when reprobate sons and daughters venture home.

The Jews knew this:

> The Lord did not love you and choose you because you outnumbered other peoples; you were the smallest nation on earth. But the Lord loved you and wanted to keep the promise that he made to your ancestors. That is why he saved you by his great might and set you free from slavery to the king of Egypt. Remember that the Lord your God is the only God and that he is faithful.

(Deuteronomy 7:7-9)

Christians know this:

> Let us give thanks to the God and Father of our
> Lord Jesus Christ! For in our union with Christ
> he has blessed us by giving us every spiritual
> blessing in the heavenly world. Even before the
> world was made, God had already chosen us to
> be his through our union with Christ, so that we
> would be holy and without fault before him. Be-
> cause of his love God had already decided that
> through Jesus Christ he would make us his
> sons—this was his pleasure and purpose.

(Ephesians 1:3-5)

Indeed, certain texts in Scripture seem to say God chooses
good guys and rejects bad guys, welcomes sheep and rejects
goats. I have a friend who was discussing the following text
from Malachi in an adult education session:

> The Lord says to his people, "I have always
> loved you." But they reply, "How have you
> shown your love for us?" The Lord answers,
> "Esau and Jacob were brothers, but I have loved
> Jacob and his descendants, and have hated
> Esau and his descendants. I have devastated
> Esau's hill country and abandoned the land to
> wild animals."

(Malachi 1:2-3)

My friend asked the people's response to that text, "Do you
believe God loves some people and hates others?" They puz-
zled in silence for awhile. Then a man's face brightened and he
exclaimed, "I believe God loves everybody. The Jews were just
smart enough to write it down!" That is not bad exegesis or
theology. Remember, it was the goats who themselves made the
choice not to see the Lord in the hungry, thirsty, sick, naked,
stranger and prisoner. They chose not to keep tabs on and

write down the places of his presence. The Lord simply honors *their* choice. On *his* side, the Lord chooses everyone.

On the other hand, on the side of our response, the responsibilities which answer God's call, on the side of faith-response, conversion, obligations to the community, and judgment by the community in evaluating conversion, the message is:

> "The right time has come and the Kingdom of God is near! Turn away from your sins and believe the Good News!"

> (Mark 1:15)

"Turn away" often was translated by the negative and somewhat flabby word, repent. The Good News calls for much more than repentence. That is too weak a word for the Greek "metanoia." I recently read a book on conversion in which 24 authors, from theological, biblical, psychological, and ethical perspectives unpacked different dimensions of metanoia.[49] I have lifted synonyms which various authors used for conversion and placed them in Figure 5.

FIGURE 5 LANGUAGE ABOUT CONVERSION

about-face
new beginning
whirling-about
other-worldly falling in
    love
self-transcendence
total being-in-love
break with the past
conscientisation
transformation
total personal revolution
shattered, crucified self
escape from the prison of
    self possession to
    possession by the Holy
    Spirit

change in the hot place of
    consciousness
self-surrender
relaxing, yielding, falling
    back on a larger Power
rapaidation of growth
unification of a divided
    self
change of direction
submission
admission of
    powerlessness
total orientation of life
    toward God
peak-experience

waking up, rising from
   sleep
counter-movement
great awakening
turning around
a new life
revolving, reversing
change, transposition
change of heart
renunciation and a new
   start
walking in the right
   direction
circumcision of the heart
turn to the reign of God
new orientation of life
act of faith
true justice
to be regenerated, to
   receive grace
twice-born

decisive joining of a
   fellowship
periodic return
self-acceptance and
   reaching beyond
passage from need to
   desire
Yes to God's gift of
   ourselves
openness to a gift
breaking through wall of
   resistance in freedom
choice for life
abandonment of our own
   security
contrition, metanoia,
   justification as event,
   fides qua
acceptance of our
   inescapable orientation
   toward mystery
great return home
   spiritual upheaval,
   integration

Love the Lord your God with all your heart, with
all your soul, and with all your mind. . . . Love
your neighbor as yourself.

(Matthew 22:37, 39)

Let the dead bury their own dead. You go and
proclaim the Kingdom of God.

(Luke 9:60)

Jesus said to them, "Anyone who starts to plow
and then keeps looking back is of no use for the
Kingdom of God."

(Luke 9:62)

There is no doubt that the first word is Good News about the Kingdom of God's love. There is also no doubt the news is so good that the response demanded is total.

There is also no doubt that there is a long history of the Christian community "binding and loosing" and making judgments about the authenticity of conversion. Bernard Cooke has called this the ministry of judgment.[50] At its worst, that has meant inquisition and witch hunts. At its best, it has been spiritual direction—helping a person evaluate (draw forth the values in her/his life) and make decisions.

Who, then, are the elect? Who shall be chosen? Decisions should always be made honoring the tension between God's impassioned choice and con-version (turning-toward us) and the need for change in us as signs of our conversion and turning toward God.

To honor God's choice, bring to focus all we have said about: the infinite worth of every person (the entire atmosphere should be one of warmth, love and respect) and the unique character of every spiritual journey (what might not be tremendous conversion for one person could well be an "about-face" for another). The person must have no doubt that God's love is always reaching out to him or her. The only question is, at what levels can I respond?

To honor our choice, bring to focus earlier discussions of faith and conversion. Lonergan's categories might help. The key conversion is religious (from life-as-problem to life-as-gift). In the RCIA process I would presume theistic and Christic conversion will be part of this (God is for me and Jesus is his gift). With the presumption that so many candidates have shoddy self-images, I suggest a critical area of discernment will be: is life gift? Is God the giver? Is Jesus living proof? To paraphrase Leonard Bernstein's lyrics in *Mass*: the question is not so much, "Do I believe in God?" but "Does God believe in me, and can I believe in me because God does?"

A second critical area for discernment will be ecclesial conversion (from the Church as "they" to the Church as "we"). Is this community the gift of God? Is this the sacred space in which the love of God and Jesus gets enfleshed? With presumptions about the bad experiences of many people with the Church as institution, and with presumptions about the need for the entire Church to move more from "they" to "we," I suggest these are serious questions.

The spiritual director will help the candidates ask these questions of themselves. More important here than at acceptance into the catechumenate, however, is the role of the community. The community celebrates and expresses God's choice. That is the positive thrust here. If that choice is to be heartfelt, the community must in some way know and love the candidate as God does. That will be the particular joy of the special ministers (catechist, spiritual director, and especially the sponsors); but there is also the responsibility of the parish assembly and the parish leadership to be more than passive "electors." Through the earlier rites and gatherings in the RCIA process, they should be part of the candidates' lives.

Before the Rite of Election, then, the catechumenal community will meet to discern, Who are the elect? That community will include: catechist, priest, sponsors, the director of the RCIA for the parish, and certainly the candidates themselves. If that prayerful discernment is put into dialogue with the candidates' personal discernment and decision, if all is done in the context of the joy of expressing God's choice and the Lord's care for different people at different stages in their journey, election should be a positive experience even for egalitarian Americans.[51]

2. Who are the Ministers?

The ministries already discussed continue in appropriate ways during this period. Ideally, catechetical sessions will have been completed so that the ministry of catechists would continue primarily after the Service of the Word on Sundays. This will leave more time for concentration on prayer, spiritual direction, and days of retreat. During this period the spotlight turns on bishop, spiritual director, and priest.

The Ministry of the Bishop. The RCIA says: "It is for the bishop, in person or through his delegate, to set up, regulate, and promote the pastoral formation of catechumens and to admit the candidates to their election and to the sacraments. It is to be hoped that, if possible, presiding at the Lenten liturgy, he will himself celebrate the rite of election and, at the Easter Vigil, the sacraments of initiation" (*RCIA*, n. 44).

Bishop Dingman of Des Moines comments: "I am convinced that the bishop could use his limited time and energies much more effectively than he does presently. Let us assume that the bishop is relieved of his responsibility for confirming children. What would happen if a bishop were to see a large part of his ministry in terms of involvement in the whole catechumenal process outlined in the RCIA?"[52]

As with all things Catholic, "the buck (of the RCIA) stops here" with the bishop. That could be just one more burden on the episcopal shoulders, or it could be seen as a way of drawing into unity a good number of episcopal priorities presently on the scene.

There have been Roman synods of bishops on evangelization and on catechesis. The RCIA can be a gathering point for much of what is going on in both areas. The U.S. bishops have some major projects going: evangelization, the Parish Project, the Year of the Family. The RCIA is bound up heart and soul with evangelization. I shall suggest later, since the RCIA *process* is a model for growth in community and also individual adult growth, it can be a starting point and model for parish renewal and also growth in our families. The Call to Action bicentennial gatherings could have had more ownership by both the bishops and the entire American Church if it had followed the RCIA model of gathering people in small communities of faith to tell their stories, raise their questions, and determine their needs. That is precisely what materials for the Year of the Family suggest.

More concretely, the bishop might begin his public involvement in the RCIA by celebrating the Rite of Election with all the catechumens in the diocese on the first Sunday of Lent. The sacraments of initiation might best be celebrated in the parishes, but there could be a celebration with the bishop at the cathedral around Pentecost as part of the mystagogical rejoicing.

During pastoral visitations the bishop could meet with the catechumens. Preparation for the ministries of the RCIA might best be handled on a diocesan and interparochial level, and the bishop can see that resources are provided. Bishop Remi DeRoo of Victoria, B.C., has launched an impressive process of training for people he calls "prayer-companions." Their "job description" is much like that of the spiritual director and also the sponsor in the RCIA, and he hopes to invite these prayer-companions into the RCIA process. At this point in history, of course, a major task of the bishop will be to help his priests appreciate the RCIA, partly through workshops but more especially through diocesan celebrations and diocesan models of the process.[53]

The Ministry of Spiritual Director. The RCIA says:

"During this period, a more intense preparation of the mind, which involves spiritual recollection more than catechesis, is intended to purify minds and hearts by the examination of conscience and by repentance and also to enlighten those minds and hearts by a deeper knowledge of Christ the Savior" (_RCIA_, n. 24).

That kind of preparation puts the spotlight on the need for spiritual directors.

For many American Catholics, and for many priests, direction (like election) carries negative overtones. In these Rogerian times of empathy, unconditional positive regard, facilitating and enabling rather than directing, the word "direction" can be out of sync.

The first gift of the spiritual director, however, is not telling but listening: helping a person listen to what the Lord is saying in his or her life. The roles are much like those of witness and guide which we saw as the roles of sponsors.

Here the _witnessing_ may simply take on greater depth with a director who may have had more experience listening to many lives. Also, the spiritual director will be at more "distance" from the candidate than the sponsor. For that reason, the spiritual director might offer greater freedom when the person is deciding to participate or not in the Rite of Election.

The director during this period will also act as *guide*, not just into the life of the parish as does the sponsor, but guide into the ways of prayer.

Some priests have had negative experiences of spiritual direction; others feel incapable. Still others rejoice in being freed by other ministers in the Church today to discover the role of the priest, in addition to being liturgical celebrant, is primarily that of spiritual director.

The Ministry of Priest. Aidan Kavanagh says: "The role of the ordained minister is mainly one of oversight, especially if he is a presbyter. As a rule, the parish priests's efforts should be directed at establishing the catechumenate, staffing it with the best persons representing a wide variety of gifts relative to conversion therapy and instruction, and over-seeing its continuing function throughout the year.... As such, his ministry is as modest as it is crucial: it is to preach wisely and well, to oversee with a firm but circumspect prudence, to preside simply and without pretense at worship, to care deeply for his people, to judge justly in fear and trembling, and to respect and foster charisms in others for the building up of the Church. He is the main facilitator in the local Church, not a living clot of surrogates for everything it must do for itself as the Body of Christ."[54]

The current cliche is that the priest's conversion is from one-man band to orchestra leader, helping each person play a part. With the present state of affairs, I think a better image is circus master who tries his best to be sure there is something going on in all three rings.

In any event, whether he is discerning gifts of musicians for an orchestra or clowns for the circus, his role is to foster charisms in others, to help others see the gifts of their God—and that is precisely spiritual direction! Then, as the man with oversight, the man who has some sense of the whole picture, who has helped old and young, rich and poor, married and single, ministers in the RCIA and outside the RCIA discover the presence of the Lord in their lives, he can gather all those folks together as unifier and reconcilier to share their stories of faith in homily and celebrate their dyings and risings in eucharist. That is why priest is celebrant.

3. What are the Liturgies and the Catechesis?

Liturgies of this period begin with the Rite of Election which launches catechumens into the time of illumination just as the Rite of Becoming Catechumens invited inquirers into the catechumenate. Just as with inquirers who decided not to take the step, there should certainly be times of prayer with those who decide to spend more time in the catechumenate.

If this Rite of Election is celebrated at the cathedral with the bishop, there should be a parish celebration earlier in the week at which the elect enroll their names in the Book of the Elect and also sign a scroll which is presented to the bishop along with scrolls from the other parishes.

We hope by this time both the candidates and the sponsors will be more free to express in public what the Lord has been doing in their lives. The rite gives the freedom to move beyond the stilted replies of the ritual and offer personal testimony of dying and rising. Not only godparents but the entire assembly may give witness to what has happened on the journey.

The most striking feature of the liturgy of election is the insistence on testimony from all parties involved. No other Roman liturgical experiences are designed like a church meeting.[55]

The rite celebrated with the bishop brings the candidates into union with the universal Church represented in his person. Often the presence of other candidates from a wide spectrum of urban, rural, suburban and different ethnic communities in the diocese also expands vision beyond narrow parish boundaries. In turn, the bishop supports and ratifies the efforts of local churches to proclaim the Good News.

The Scrutinies. Here there may be a case for a name change. Perhaps Rites of Healing might hit the mark, or "a long careful look" at our lives. The Scripture readings for these three Sundays in Lent are always taken from cycle A. There is the Samaritan woman who asks for a cup of water and experiences the healing of the Lord who is Living Water not only to her but to her townsfolk in Samaria. There is the blind man who needs 20/20 vision and learns of Pharisees more blind than he ever was, in desperate need of healing by the Lord who is Light of the World. There are Martha and Mary weeping outside a stench-filled tomb, asking that their brother might live again and receiving the healing message of the Lord who is the Resurrection and the Life and who promises life eternal.

Each of these rites extends a healing touch to the elect where they are most in need of cleansing, of the light of faith, and of resurrection. And the entire assembly stands with them, both to promise healing and to experience healing where they are most broken and wounded. They are represented by the sponsors who stand with the elect, with hands on their shoulders, offering the touch of support and healing.

We have looked at the Presentations of the Creed and the Lord's Prayer, which can be offered during the catechumenate or during Lent. The final prescribed rites for this period are the *Pre-vigil Rites* (profession of faith, opening of ears and mouth, choosing a Christian name, anointing with oil of catechumens). The "ephpheta" and the anointing can be done also during the catechumenate. The point here is that the RCIA recommends that the elect gather, perhaps with an invitation to the parish, earlier in the day on Holy Saturday to pray together and share their anticipation of the night to come.

Note: during all these rites and certainly in the sacraments of initiation, there are times for clear distinctions between those baptized and those who are not. The baptized will also want to celebrate stages in their journey, so they should have appropriate expressions of God's love and their faith.

The opposite situation may occur on Holy Saturday. During the time of prayer early in the day, the baptized may celebrate the sacrament of Reconciliation. Many unbaptized express the need for a similar experience of healing. They should be given the chance to open up their lives with a spiritual director and celebrate forgiveness and "shalom" in some appropriate way.

The Sacraments of Initiation. I do not intend to walk through these rites which are so familiar. Just two points:

First, the sacraments of initiation are Baptism-Confirmation-Eucharist, one integral celebration. I shall return to this when we discuss infant baptism and also confirmation.

Second, the vigil service offers another example in which the liturgical structure is not so solid. The present order gets us all fired up with paschal candle and exsultet, then tells us to settle down for readings, then wants us on fire again with Gospel. A better structure would be to begin in darkness and quiet with Old Testament readings; process to another place following Christ, the Light of the World, imaged in fire and praised in exsultet; feel our hearts burning within us with the proclamation of the Gospel of Resurrection, surrounded by climactic "alleluia's"; celebrate with our brothers and sisters their entry into that mystery of death and life through Baptism-Confirmation-Eucharist.

Catechesis. James Parker suggests that during precatechumenate and catechumnate the one searching for meaning may experience especially intellectual and moral conversion when meanings and values fall into place. The person may be less conscious that it has always been God who has been searching for her or him.

"Less dramatically does he experience conversion as God's gracious choice of him. There comes a time, however, for him to experience conversion as just that—the work of God, the work of one who has sought him out, found him, and grasped him. Such an experience is what is meant by religious conversion, or conversion in its specifically religious dimension. It is the experience of being grasped by ultimate concern, of God's love flooding our hearts. Religious conversion, in short, is the experience of conversion as election."[56]

In response to grace, and in freedom, conversion in its multiple dimensions is happening throughout the RCIA process. I mentioned above, however, that religious conversion is at the center of what is celebrated in the Rite of Election. Lent is a time to unfold what has been celebrated. If there has been an extended and leisurely catechumenate, we shall not be squeezing into Lent catechetical sessions which should have been completed by this time. The RCIA calls this a time more of spiritual recollection (re-collecting all that has happened) than catechesis. The elect relax their searching and ponder the mystery that they are elect, that God has searched them out and chosen them. Lent is an appropriate time for the re-collecting. It has always been a time spent in the desert with Hebrews and with Jesus when Yahweh purifies and heals and enlightens both Jews and Jesus. They become servants of the Lord who experience their own emptiness, weakness, and powerlessness but who are also overwhelmed and grasped by the saving power of the Father. Lent is a time for the elect to enter the desert.

Lenten Retreat. The Church begins Lent in the desert with Jesus on the first Sunday. A retreat early in Lent sets the tone for the entire period. Members of the catechumenal community may be part of the retreat, perhaps those initiated the previous year who might share how their journey has continued, perhaps members of the parish. There must be private time for the elect, however, to meet the Lord who is offering life.[57]

Spiritual Direction. The retreat experience is extended through regular meetings with a spiritual director during the weeks of Lent.

Journal-keeping. I recommend keeping a journal during the precatechumenate so that people can keep track of their story. Lent would be time to re-collect the stories and to discern more clearly the Lord as the principal actor. Jim Parker calls this a decentering of self (from a narcissistic story).[58]

Celebrations of the Word. The elect continue to meet to ponder God's Word after their dismissal at Sunday Eucharist. That Word plus the interpretations by sponsor and the elect give the individual more to re-collect during the following week.

The Life of the Parish. The elect share in whatever the wider community does during Lent, when appropriate. This includes the usual practices of penance, prayer, fasting, and alms giving.

6. The Period of Mystagogia

> I send you to shake the sleepers
> to wake the dead, to say
> past, present and future are solved
> in life's single thrust
> in the power-dance of atoms
> broken and re-assembled
> of bones stripped and fleshed anew.
> To live forever, never to die:
> such is the human craving
> the dream drifting from age to age
> formless as mist in fields of air.
> I send you to announce
> a deathless world emerging
> from the sea of transformation
> rising to the morning light.
> The winter is past beloved
> the night is over: wake
> from your ancestral fears
> and see the empty grave, the folded linen
> the darkness rolled away.
> You live, you are alive.
> Fear not:
> I am with you always
> until the end of the world.[39]

It is paschal time, Easter-Pentecost and forever. It is the time when the dead awake with stripped bones and new flesh. It is time to drink and savor new wine. It is time to live the dream, to announce winter is past, night is over, and fear is gone because Jesus is with us until the end of the journey.

1. Who are the Neophytes?

With rare exceptions, in days gone by, neophytes were those abandoned at the font. "Ex opere operato" sin was washed away; they were children of God. "See you in Church."

Not only neophytes but the entire parish after the penance of Lent and the hustle-bustle of Holy Week breathed a sigh of relief, "Thank God that's over!" The clergy took off on well-deserved vacations. All sorts of professional religious groups scheduled conventions. Schools and CCD prepared to close. And neophytes drifted off into the night.

Some of the above is a "cheap shot." Paschal time is party time. Vacations and conventions are often great parties. *If* they sent us back refreshed to celebrate with neophytes and the parish, they were good mystagogia. Usually they were just a good escape. Therefore, I assert that more than any other period in the RCIA, the time of mystagogia confronts present pastoral practice head-on.

Who are the neophytes? A better way to phrase the question is—what are the neophytes doing? Where are they going? Psychologist Erik Erikson, the father of the so-called adolescent identity crisis, once complained that although the question was placed in his mouth, he never asked, "Who am I?" He said identity is not discovered by looking in the mirror but by looking out into our relationships. The proper questions are, "Where am I going? What gifts do I have to give?"

That is how the RCIA describes neophytes.

"The community and the neophytes move forward together, meditating on the Gospel, sharing in the eucharist, and performing works of charity" (*RCIA*, n. 37).

What are they doing? Where are they going? They are continuing the Emmaus journey (one of the first Gospels they hear after initiation). They have met the Risen Lord on the road. He continues to open up the Word to them. They recognize him in the breaking of bread. And they charge forth with hearts burning within them to share the Good News in charity. Gospel—eucharist—charity (cf. Luke 24:13-35).

Gospel. Neophytes are those who now have a Good News story. We began to speak of stories during the precatechumenate period. It is quite possible that the entire RCIA process is moving from *stories* to *Story*, from fragments to wholeness, pericopes to Gospel. Without our permission, persons may enter the precatechumenate fully integrated. The presumption is that they do not and that the entire RCIA process has been one of putting together the fragments: the individual events of their own lives, the lives in our living Tradition of Jesus and his people, the lives of the catechumenal community which is sharing faith—so that all of this is experienced as one Story of dying and rising. That is the story neophytes just celebrated in the sacraments of Easter initiation. Now on their Emmaus journey they are unpacking the meaning.

Tom Downs writes:

> Objectively speaking, story is simply a narrative that links various sequences. Subjectively and to the point, to have a story is to be a person. Or to turn the phrase, to be a person is to have a story. . . . Without my story, I have no identity. I do not know who I am, or what I am about. "If you have no story, how do you know where you're going; and if you're going somehwere, how will you know when you get there?"[60]

Well, neophytes have a story. They knew where they were going—Easter. They knew when they got there, and now during a life of mystagogia (penetrating deeper into the mystery of dying and rising) they continue the journey of deepening conversion on the way to Emmaus. They are integrated. The rhythms will differ; Story stays the same.

Eucharist. Neophytes are those who make eucharist, who "give thanks." Having discovered Good News, having experienced that their individual stories are part of the Story of God, they pause in their journey to gather round the table and give thanks to the Lord. Now they know he has been with them every step of the way. Now they know that all their risings were not their own production and that they do not write the final chapter. They have been decentered of self and recentered on God—so they worship, they give thanks in the breaking of the bread.

Charity. Neophytes are those with hearts burning within them who share Good News so others might give thanks. Call it witness. Call it service. Call it ministries. Whatever the term, neophytes are those who have discerned the gifts of God in their lives and know that gifts are for-giving.

Does it sound unreal? Well, Easter is a time for dreams! And at one parish last Easter, some of those dreams got enfleshed in the following reactions by the neophytes:

"The Easter Vigil was top dog!"

"It was euphoric!"

"It was the most beautiful experience of my life!"

"I felt that I was really welcomed. . . that people were happy to have me join their church."[61]

2. Who are the Ministers?

All of the above—all the ministries we have already discussed.

The *community* welcomes and celebrates. The *catechist* helps the neophytes unpack the meaning of the celebrations. The *spiritual director* helps neophytes listen to the Lord, discern their gifts, and offer them in service. The *priest* celebrates and prays. The *bishop* celebrates and prays; we hope there might be a diocesan celebration for all the neophytes and perhaps an anniversay reunion celebration for all who were initiated in recent years.

The critical ongoing ministry is *sponsoring*, the continuing support from a sponsoring community and from the sponsor (godparent) delegated by that community to continue the journey through mystagogia and beyond with the new Christian.

A second crucial ministry is that of the *neophytes* to the wider community and especially to new inquirers. With the excitement and wonder of children at the beach for the first time or at their first big birthday party, the newborn Catholics cut through the dullness and boredom and upset the routine which too often marks the lives of born Catholics. During the Sunday Eucharists of paschal time, often in words that stammer and falter but always with a sincerity that is clear and compelling, the neophytes share with the whole community what the Lord is doing in them. The homilist and sponsors can help them with stories, but even the most shy people seem to find the nerve after Easter. In one case, a woman, who always ran for cover when she had to do anything in public, after initiation said, "I simply have to tell these people what has been happening in my life!"

The special ministry of neophytes is to new inquirers who might join them in some of their reflection sessions to learn what happens on the journey. This can launch inquirers on their own RCIA journey at Pentecost.

3. What are the Liturgies and the Catechesis?

Aidan Kavanagh describes mystagogical catechesis: "It raises the organism to a peak of physical and psychic coordination where it 'knows' to a degree never otherwise attainable. The dog 'points' its game; the wrestler prepares to attack; the blind touch and thus 'see'; the mystic moves from mere meditation into pure contemplation; lovers exclude all else in their mutual gaze. The Church baptizes. The senses of touch, sight, smell, hearing, and taste lose their separateness to fuse into one state of perception. The eye penetrates the icon; smell ingests the tongue as the ears devour its sound. Perception fuses in space with time, and a thing is not just known but possessed with so indelible an intensity that it will never be forgotten. But it can never be put into words alone."[62]

That includes these words. You will not learn about the RCIA from my words. You have to know it with a Hebrew understanding of knowledge; you have to have "intercourse" with the experience. You have to drink the wine.

In that sense, the catechesis of the entire RCIA process is mystagogical. First, the experience. Then, reflection to unpack its meaning.

One way to look at this is to distinguish between primary process and secondary process thinking. Figure 6 shows the physiology which situates primary processes in the right lobe of the brain (which controls the left side of the body and is called "left-handed" thinking) and secondary processes in the left lobe of the brain (and is called "right-handed" thinking).

Left-handed thinking plays in the world of imagination, symbol, intuition, feeling and is in immediate contact with our experience. Right-handed thinking is one step removed from our experience and analyzes what has happened. Left-handed thinking produces art, poetry, hunches and lucky guesses, myth and story. Right-handed thinking produces principles, logic, and theologies which analyze stories and develop abstractions and meanings. Left-handed thinking is holistic and weds unconscious and conscious, body and spirit, all the senses with all our reflections. Right-handed thinking breaks things into parts and delights in Cartesian "clear and distinct ideas." I have suggested that to avoid literalism, for example, regarding both Scripture and doctrine, we need to analyze, critique, and break things into parts with right-handed thinking. The challenge is: can Humpty Dumpty put it back together again?

Right-handed thinking lives in space and time. Left-handed thinking lives in mystery and eternity. Liturgies thrive in the world of the left-handed.[63] Catechesis thrives in both right and left but begins and ends in the left.

That is often the movement and rhythm of the RCIA process. Ideally, it begins with left-handed thinking about stories, moves more toward the right during the catechumenate with reflections about the stories, and swings back to the left during mystagogia when the starting point is the symbols and experiences in liturgy.

The mystagogical principles insist: the first Word is not words. Since Vatican II, we have had a passion for understanding. People complain that the vernacular destroyed the mystery of Latin. In a sense, they are right—but the wonder-ful language of Shakespeare and Gerard Manley Hopkins does not destroy. Verbiage destroys. The endless commentaries of mouthy "cele-

Figure #6

EQUAL RIGHTS FOR
BOTH HEMISPHERES OF THE BRAIN

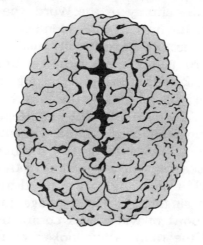

Left Hemisphere (Right side of body)	Right Hemisphere (Left side of body)
Speech/Verbal	Spatial/Musical
Logical, Mathematical	Holistic
Linear, Detailed	Artistic, Symbolic
Sequential	Simultaneous
Controlled	Emotional
Intellectual	Intuitive, Creative
Dominant	Minor (Quiet)
Worldly	Spiritual
Active	Receptive
Analytic	Synthetic, Gestalt
Reading, Writing, Naming	Facial Recognition
Sequential Ordering	Simultaneous Comprehension
Perception of Significant Order	Perception of Abstract Patterns
Complex Motor Sequences	Recognition of Complex Figures

Clinical and experimental evidence along with anthropological data
are outlining the separate functions of the hemispheres.

brants" who tell people what they are now going to experience when they stand, sit, and kneel destroy. Speaking about symbols before they can speak for themselves destroys.

Mystagogia says: let the symbols speak. Pere Joseph Gelineau tells the following story of an Easter Vigil in his church: "At the end of the Liturgy of the Word, the paschal candle was brought into the nave in total silence. (When you want to make a liturgical gesture which really means something, you cannot say a word. Before or after the gesture, yes. But never while you are making that gesture.) In our church there is a long room which runs parallel to the nave. . . Two people began to walk from the nave into this parallel room. Others followed and the procession continued with the singing of the litany of the saints. The room next to the nave had been left in total darkness, except for a spotlight in the ceiling directly over a large bowl of water. As they entered the room, the two leaders stopped singing. . . . The passage through the dark room with the bowl of water was completely silent. When people entered the room, they looked at the water; some made the sign of the cross, some drank, some sprinkled themselves or splashed water over their heads; some did nothing. After the Easter Vigil I got a lot of reactions. But the one which always came first was, 'I was overwhelmed when I passed through the room with the water.' Why? Precisely because there was no explanation, no pre-established meaning given to the bowl of water. Everyone had to find a meaning given to the bowl of water. Everyone had to find a meaning in this event, to situate themselves in relation to it, to take a stand."[64]

Last year on the Second Sunday of the Passion, Charles Bordenca, the pastor of a parish in Birmingham, Alabama, says his worship committee placed a table in the center aisle of the Church, covered it with a red cloth, and placed thorns, spikes, and a lash. The people processed by the table. Not a word was said. Let the symbols speak and the people respond in their own way.

Al Benavides, pastor of St. Timothy's Parish in San Antonio, tells of how previous to his coming a new church had been built; and an ultra-modern wrought iron crucifix had replaced a crucifix dearly loved by his Mexican-American people. They passed the old crucifix from home to home and developed liturgies around it. When Al arrived, he received hundreds of requests to put the crucifix back in the church. They celebrated a "welcome home" of the crucifix with the bishop and over a thousand people attending, full of smiles and tears of joy.

"I became aware that the controversy had actually become a symbolic conflict. It was no longer merely a question of the crucifix. It was now a question of who the church belonged to. What the people were asking for was a church in which they could feel comfortable, in which they would be accepted as they are with their foibles and imperfections."[65]

The Jesus of the people was welcomed home. The symbol spoke. The people did not need to be told how to respond. Mystagogia![66]

The period of mystagogia is jammed with this kind of liturgy-catechesis. Let the symbols speak, and then reflect together on their response. The term mystagogia (literally, learning the mysteries) comes from the Fathers and gives the key to this period: entering more deeply into the mysteries of dying and rising. In the liturgical celebrations the neophytes are participating in those mysteries; it is there that the symbols grasp them and draw them toward the Lord. Catechesis will help them express what they have experienced in those symbolic encounters.

This was the approach of Cyril of Jerusalem. For the neophytes his sessions included: The Mysteries, On Baptism, On Chrism, On the Body and Blood of Christ, On the Sacred Liturgy and communion. Following that approach, we would not squeeze in sacramental catechesis before Easter. Certainly, because catechumens will have sacramental questions, especially about Reconciliation and Eucharist, some sacramental catechesis will have to be done during the catechumenate. But for most sacramental reflection, we would wait until the neophytes at Easter and paschal time are surrounded with water, burning candle, white garment, oil, bread and wine, alleluia, and a risen people. What have all these sights, sounds, smells and touches done to them?

This demands, of course, integral, credible, and robust symbols. After Eucharist, for example, we can take out paragraph 7 of the *Constitution on the Liturgy* and *tell* people that Christ is really present in Word, meal, ministers and people. If the Word is muttered from a disposable missalette, if it is more difficult to believe that this is really bread than this is really Christ, if the ministers are only clerics playing mechanically in a one-man band, and if the people are "really present" only to their private concerns—they may leave with a stronger experience of real absence. If faith is present in proclamation of Word, genuine communion present in the sharing of bread and wine, self-giving service present in ministers, and shared lives present in people—then we have a starting point for sacramental catechesis.

In a sense, the RCIA process has been offering other starting points from the very beginning. This period is building on what has already been experienced, not just other symbols but the journeys. The process was one of discerning that the Lord has always been really present on that journey at times of dying and rising, healing, reconciliation, love and communion. Every sacrament celebrates that paschal journey and reveals that outside liturgy there are sacramental moments which are charged with the presence of the Lord. Liturgy celebrates all those moments.

Some concluding "nuts and bolts" observations: sacramental catechesis in part happens within liturgy, especially at homily time when neophytes, sponsors, catechists, priest and the entire community share what has been happening to them when grasped by the symbols.

Sacramental catechesis continues in weekly reflection sessions. These sessions should offer some right-handed thinking: some history of liturgy, some sacramental theology.

This is a time for exposure to the many ways the Church prays. That might include the Liturgy of the Hours, devotions, introduction to prayer groups in the parish.

This is time to discern what service or ministry the neophytes might offer and to celebrate that at a Commitment Sunday.[67] One instrument I have used, by the way, which helps both with clarifying personal styles of prayer and gifts for service based on personality traits is the Myers-Briggs Personality Profile Instrument. There is some fascinating research on how different polarities in our personality affect prayer. This might help the neophytes, or it might be used earlier in the process.

I shall close with some left-handed thinking by a neophyte about a neophyte. The writer is Alice Meynell, speaking about her conversion at the turn of this century when she was age 20; she calls it "The Young Neophyte."

> Who knows what days I answer for today?
> Giving the bud I give the flower. I bow
> This yet unfaded and faded brow;
> Bending these knees and feeble knees, I pray.
>
> Thoughts yet unripe in me I bend one way,
> Give one repose to pain I know not now,
> one check to joy that comes, I guess not how.
> I dedicate my fields when Spring is grey.
>
> O rash! (I smile) to pledge my hidden wheat.
> I fold today at altars far apart
> Hands trembling with what toils? In their retreat
> I seal my love to be, my folded art.
> I light the tapers at my head and feet,
> And lay the crucifix on the silent heart.[68]

7. Implications of the RCIA

These implications are either very tentative probes or conclusions presented with little development.

IMPLICATIONS FOR OTHER SACRAMENTS

1. Infant Baptism.

The baptismal waters have calmed since Aidan Kavanagh and others claimed that adult initiation is the "norm."[69] It seems clear that this does not necessarily exclude the baptism of infants, but it does question indiscriminate infant baptism and raises other possibilities. The conversion and growth of the adult envisioned in the RCIA is the norm, and anything done earlier should contribute to that growth.

Assumptions from the RCIA process which help pastoral judgment include: every child is born in the Father's love. No liturgy brings God's love to a person for the first time. Liturgies celebrate our discovery of the Father's presence and love.

Second, every child is born into a world of evil and sin. Anthropology and developmental psychology leave us even more convinced that evil can have enormous influence on a person during the first days and months of life. (I mentioned earlier that the RCIA is weak on this.)

Third, initiation is into a community of faith which offers healing for sin and love for nourishment. This assumes some degree of ecclesial conversion on the part of parents.

Fourth, initiation into that community of faith in the RCIA takes place in periods and stages. Baptism is not the only moment. Catechumens are members of the Church.

With those assumptions as background, we have several possibilities for the initiation of infants.

First, in all three of the following options, a "catechumenal" community of faith is offered to parents and child. Their meetings would include not just the usual explanation of the rites but would follow the RCIA periods of moving from inquiry toward mystagogia. The ministers would be a sponsoring community, especially other parents and peers. With parents, the questions might begin with, "What are your hopes for your children?"

Second, parents who have a strong desire for infant baptism and whose faith is discerned by themselves and the electing community (cf. Rite of Election) might celebrate the sacraments of initiation. We should move toward the practice of the Eastern Church in this case and celebrate Baptism-Confirmation-Eucharist with infants (which does not imply that infants would regularly receive Eucharist after initiation). If this is done, there would be frequent celebrations of the renewal of initiation throughout a person's life.

Third, Aidan Kavanagh suggests a restored and intelligible initiation sequence involving: a) enrolling infants as catechumens at an early age; b) guiding them through the catechumenate in a careful progression until an age of free acceptance of Christ and his Church is determined by catechist, family, pastor and congregation; c) full initiation through Lenten observance, Baptism-Confirmation-Eucharist on Holy Saturday-Easter, and post-baptismal catechesis through that Eastertide.[70]

My difficulty with this is in determining the "age of free acceptance" and in tying initiation for children to any "age of maturity." Does that also exclude children from Eucharist until then?

Fourth, enrollment of children as catechumens at an early age (as above) and celebration of Baptism-Confirmation-Eucharist when the child joins the wider community at the table of the Lord; for many children, that would take place at 6-9 years of age at a time of transition when the child is moving from family into school and a wider community. This approach would also include celebrations which deepen and renew initiation-conversion at appropriate times in the person's life, with provision for a special renewal when the person enters adult responsibilities in the Church.

Note: I realize all of these options create pastoral problems with people who learned well about limbo or who want to keep their children coming to classes to prepare for Confirmation. These issues demand sensitive ministers who spend time with people. But in view of the problems with the present practice, it is time to move.[71]

2. Confirmation.

I simply make my own the conclusions of John Roberto's fine NCDD research paper of 1979:

"If a reform and renewal of our pastoral practice along the lines of the *Rite of Christian Initiation of Adults* is to take place, a quantum leap in pastoral practice is called for on theological, sociological, psychological and pastoral grounds. Theologically, the RCIA's understanding of the Sacraments of Initiation and their intimate connection leads one to a reevaluation of a theology which views them as separate entities, and views confirmation as the sacrament of Christian maturity. Liturgically, the RCIA reestablishes a process and ritual-celebration for Christian initiation. Sociologically, our current pastoral practice relies upon a predominately Christian culture. Such culture no longer exists and we live in an age of pluralism; and thus there is an urgent need to reestablish a catehumenal structure in which Christians are made. Psychologically, the maturity debate has left us frustrated; what is now called for is a way of viewing faith development within the context of a community of faith. Lastly, our pastoral practice has not lived up to the expectations placed upon it. We still suffer from the large disaffection of youth and young adults who have been confirmed and are no longer active in the Church. We still suffer from inactive adult Catholics, despite all the adult education programs that are offered."[72]

Two comments. First, in view of the above, it is time to confront head-on those who claim that the restoration of Baptism-Confirmation-Eucharist as one rite of initiation is archaic and not good pastoral practice. They have co-opted the word "pastoral"; but it should be clear by now that to tie Confirmation as a separate "maturity rite" to any time in early or late adolescence is pastoral nonsense. Perhaps we need to celebrate a "puberty rite of passage," but let us not load that baggage onto Confirmation.

Second, I think better pastoral practice would be to celebrate full initiation with children rather early (presuming a community of faith in family around them) and then "confirm" that initiation through celebrations at important passage points in their journey, tapping the various dimensions of the RCIA process.

This is an approach taken by several Christian churches (cf. the *Proposed Book of Common Prayer* of 1976, the *Lutheran Book of Worship* of 1978, and the Methodist *Service of Baptism, Confirmation, and Renewal* of 1976). Daniel Stevick, who helped put together the Episcopal rite, speaks of Confirmation A and Confirmation B which express the conflicts in understanding Confirmation:

Confirmation A	Confirmation B
sacramental rite	catechetical rite
Holy Spirit as gift	renewal of baptismal promises
something God does	something we do
initiatory	not initiatory
non-repeatable	repeatable

early Church (Rome)   late Middle Ages
after split of baptism
and confirmation

The Roman Catholic confirmation rite has tried to save something of both meanings. These other churches in Confirmation A celebrate an integral initiation restoring the unity of water, oil, and bread/wine. Confirmation B is celebrated at important moments, possibly including the acceptance of adult responsibilities in the church and puberty; but the times are left to the creativity of the local church and the grace of God.

3. Marriage.

Just two comments and a question. Sacramental marriage often happens at the beginning of a process of conversion to God and union with each other. Too often, on the one hand, the wedding "mystagogia" precedes the storytelling and inquiry, the growth in a community of faith, and conversion to God and each other. Full initiation in sacraments in the RCIA, on the other hand, happens at the end of a process marked by appropriate liturgical celebrations along the way which celebrate a deepening union in covenant. What if our celebration of marriage took seriously the RCIA process?

4. Sacramental Preparation.

If the RCIA process is the normal way of deepening our conversion into the dying and rising of Jesus, and if every sacrament celebrates the mystery of that dying and rising, the RCIA process is a norm for all sacramental preparation.

IMPLICATONS FOR PARISH RENEWAL

At the International Symposium on the Catechumenate in France, I was interested (and discouraged) to hear that many of the movements which brought life to the French Church of the 50s and 60s were dead. Parishes in many cases are also dead, but before he died Paul VI urged French bishops to turn once again to the parishes which might offer a more stable ongoing source of renewal for French Catholics.

During recent years, our own country has experienced exciting renewal of religious life in certain movements, especially Marriage Encounter, charismatic renewal, and Cursillo. Many of them have ingredients of the RCIA process, and many of them are making increased efforts to put people in touch with their parishes.

The RCIA, however, is part and parcel of parish life and touches people who look to parish as their normal and most frequent experience of a community of faith. Especially in the ministries and the liturgies, the entire community is caught up in the process of conversion.

Two comments. First, the RCIA should not be tamed or diverted from its primary focus of initiating new Catholics. It should not become just another instrument for adult education or updating. That should be a separate though related track.

Second, the RCIA process, however, can be a norm for evaluating the ingredients of that second track and for other efforts at total parish renewal. Programs such as *Renew* from the Archdiocese of Newark, *Christ Renews the Parish* from Cleveland, and materials developed for parish renewal by Father Chuck Gallagher have some of the RCIA ingredients. More explicitly, my own experience is with several parishes in the diocese of Richmond which have implemented the RCIA for several years and are now offering sessions modeled after the four periods for all Catholics in the parish.

Figure 7 outlines the dimensions of that process as it was designed by the staff of Our Lady of Nazareth Parish in Roanoke, Virginia. All of the adults and high school students were invited to a "total parish learning experience" which was a kick-off for each period. At that time they received a home study guide prepared by parish staff and parishioners; this guide offered an explanation of the period, plus testimony written by parishioners (e.g., faith stories and conversion stories), plus theological, biblical, liturgical, and educational materials which could be used at home. Each of these periods offered some formal adult education sessions on the themes of the period, and

Figure #7

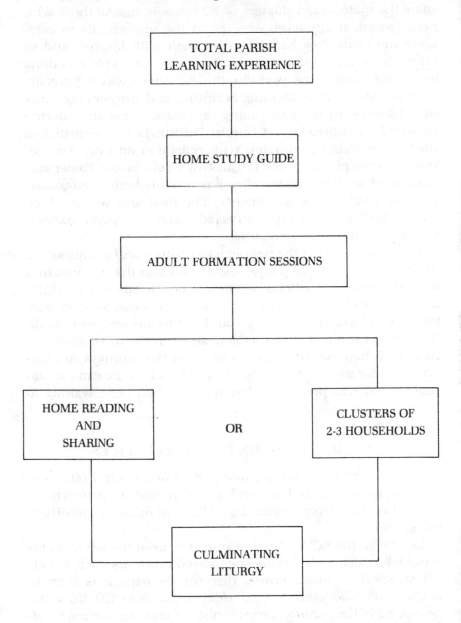

TOTAL PARISH
LEARNING EXPERIENCE

HOME STUDY GUIDE

ADULT FORMATION SESSIONS

HOME READING
AND
SHARING

OR

CLUSTERS OF
2-3 HOUSEHOLDS

CULMINATING
LITURGY

there was time either to read the home study guide privately or share the materials in clusters of 2-3 households. All those who participated, at any level, were given the opportunity to celebrate the steps they had taken on their faith journey and to enter the next period at a "culminating liturgy." This was done five times during the year. In the fall there was a "precatechumenate" period stressing Scripture and story-telling. During Advent-Christmas-Epiphany a "catechumenate" period centered on Christ and Church. During Lent the principal theme was moral conversion with reflection on Christian values. A fourth period which began two weeks before Easter and continued for three weeks after Easter launched "mystagogia" and centered on the sacraments. The final four weeks which culminated in Pentecost stressed another "mystagogical" theme—vocation and ministries.

The response from the people was positive and encouraging. At some level, over 450 people participated in the process. In a second parish, St. Nicholas in Virginia Beach, 60% of the adults in the parish have enrolled in the same process. Most important, it was based in the parish (and not in movements outside the parish); and it received its genesis from the RCIA itself. Parishioners had observed and celebrated the journeys of catechumens for several years. They began to ask, "Why can't we do that?" That was precisely what the staff had been waiting to hear.

IMPLICATIONS FOR DIOCESAN OFFICES

My perception is that the most effective diocesan offices of religious education and of worship see themselves primarily as committed to ministry formation. They are ministers ministering to ministers.

Central to the RCIA is shared ministry, from the whole community but also with various specialized ministers such as catechist, sponsor, and spiritual director. Perhaps it is time to begin to offer diocesan services today just as the CCD did at the beginning of the century for catechists of children—namely, offer resources for the training of RCIA ministers for parishes on an interparochial level. Ralph Keifer writes: "The working model of a catechumenate in the church is based on the diocese, not the local parish. We may have problems making that work in our mammoth dioceses, but the model should be seen as something of a challenge with some very practical implications. One of these is the development of interparochial ministries; getting parishes to share resouces, the human ones especially, as they build catechumenates. For one thing, few parishes today have enough persons preparing for baptism to allow for the individual parish to form all the ministries and do all the work necessary. The situation cries out for clusters of some kind to share in developing a catechumenate, yet without the catechumens losing a sense of the local church where they will live."[73]

William Bauman describes such a three-parish effort in the diocese of Kansas City-Saint Joesph.[74] Diocesan offices assisted in the development.

☐ Conclusion

I shall conclude where the RCIA process begins—with inquiry, in this case, the inquiry of Jesus. On their journey together, Jesus is forever asking the disciples questions. At one point he turns to Peter and asks, "Who do men say that I am?" Who do all those other people say that I am? That is what he does with inquirers and catechumens and with the rest of us in the process described in the RCIA. But then he turns to Peter and asks, "Who do *you* say that I am?" He looks us straight in the eye, throughout the journey, and says, "Don't quote your parents, or Karl Rahner, or even Matthew or Luke! Who do *you* say that I am? What does my story have to do with your story?"

Only the unique person on pilgrimage can answer that question, but the RCIA can provide a community of seekers, believers, and concelebrants singing "Alleluia!" if the person answers, "You are the Christ, the Son of the living God!" That would also call for another glass of wine!

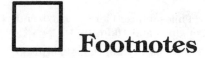# Footnotes

1 Ralph Keifer, "Christian Initiation: The State of the Question," *Worship*, 48:7, p. 402.

2 This testimony and that of the catechumen which preceded are taken from *The Chicago Catechumenate*, an excellent little publication, edited by Ronald Lewinski, published five times per year, and available from: Liturgy Training Program, 155 East Superior, Chicago, IL 60611. The publication reports both theory and practical suggestions on the RCIA. An even more elaborate pastoral guide is *Christian Initiation Resources*, published four times each year, with suggestions for each of the RCIA periods and liturgies as well as implications for evangelization, parish renewal, and sacramental preparation, available from William H. Sadlier, Inc., New York.

3 Raymond Kemp, "The Catechmenate and Parish Renewal," *New Catholic World*, 222·1329, p. 184.

4 Maurice Dingman, "The Role of the Bishop in Christian Initiation," in *Becoming a Catholic Christian*. (New York: William H. Sadlier, Inc., 1978), p. 145.

5 For a more in-depth historical treatment, cf. two books by Michel Dujarier, *A History of the Catechumenate: the First Six Centuries* and *The Rites of Christian Initiation: Historical and Pastoral Reflections*. (New York: William H. Sadlier, Inc., 1979).

6 cf. Robert Bellah, "Civil Religion in America," *Daedalus*, Winter, 1967.

7 For an excellent treatment of adult religious education cf. the NCDD research paper of Kevin Coughlin, "Motivating Adults for Religious Education." (Washington, DC: USCC Publications, 1976); a classic text in general adult education is: Malcolm Knowles, *The Modern Practice of Adult Education*. (New York: Association Press, 1970).

8 cf. Abraham Maslow's comments in *Motivation and Personality*, 2nd Edition. (New York: Harper and Row, 1959).

9 For a more extended treatment of the RCIA process as a model for adult development, cf. James Dunning, "The Rite of Christian Initiation of Adults," *Worship*, 53:2, pp. 142-156.

10 Bernard Lonergan in *Insight*. (New York: Philosophical Library, 1957), and *Method in Theology*. (London: Darton, Longman and Todd, 1971).

11 This approach and the scheme in Figure 2 are taken from Daniel Levinson with Charlotte Darrow, Edward Klein, Maria Levinson, Braxton McKee, *The Seasons of a Man's Life*. (New York: Alfred A. Knopf, 1970). Other researchers in adult development include: Roger Gould, Robert Havighurst, Jane Loevinger, Bernice Neugarten, Gail Sheehy, and George Vaillant; an excellent summary of their research is found in Vivian McCoy, Colleen Ryan, James Lichtenburg. *The Adult Cycle: Training Manual and Reader*. (Lawrence, Kansas: Adult Life Resource Center, 1978).

12 Carl Jung, *Modern Man in Search of a Soul*. (New York: Harvert Books, 1933), p. 264.

13 Lonergan, *Method in Theology*, pp. 237-243. I believe that Edward Braxton's development of the categories will soon be published in his book, *The Wisdom Community*.

14 John Shea, "Notes Toward a Theology of Ministry," *Chicago Studies*, 17:3, p. 323.

15 *Ibid.*, p. 235.

16 Tertullian, *De Baptismo*, 18:37.

17 Augustine, *Confessions*.

18 Richard C. McBrien, "The New Call to Ministry," *St. Anthony's Messenger*, March, 1979, p. 22; and "Service Plus Mission Equals Ministry," *Today's Parish*, October, 1979, pp. 43-47.

19 cf. My eight articles in PACE 8 and 9, published by St. Mary's Press in Winona, MH; collected in *Ministries: Sharing Gods Gifts*. (Winona, MN: St. Mary's Press, 1980).

20 *Ibid.*, passim.

21 I have also discussed this period in "The Stages of Initiation, 1. Inquiry," *Becoming a Catholic Christian*. (New York: William H. Sadlier, Inc., 1978), pp. 92-103.

22 Andrew Greeley, *Unsecular Man*. (New York: Schocken Books, 1972), p. 1.

23 Dietrich Bonhoeffer, *Letters and Papers from Prison*. (London: Fontana Books, 1953), p. 173.

24 John E. Smith, *Experience and God*. (New York: The Viking Press, 1968), p. 151. Smith is writing as a philosopher; the theological language is my own.

25 Andrew Greeley, *The Great Mysteries* (New York: Seabury Press, 1976).

114

26 Antoine de St. Exupery, *The Wind the Sand and the Stars*. (New York: Reynal and Hitchock, 1939), p. 23.

27 Kenneth Boyack, C.S.P., *A Parish Guide to Adult Initiation*. (Ramsey, NJ: Paulist Press, 1979).

28 Aidan Kavanagh, "Initiation," in *Simple Gifts*, Vol. II. (Washington, DC: the Liturgical Conference, 1974), pp. 12-13.

29 Jean Haldane, *Religious Pilgrimage*. (Washington, DC: the Alban Institute, 1975), p. 11.

30 NC News Service.

31 For resources both on the theory of biography as theology and the practice of storytelling through exercises and strategies, cf. my article in *Becoming a Catholic Christian*, p. 103.

32 Kevin Hart is providing suggestions for the liturgies of the RCIA in *Christian Initiation Resources*, a new periodical from William H. Sadlier, Inc.

33 Raymond Kemp offers questions which help inquirers make the decision to become catechumens in *A Journey in Faith: An Experience of the Catechumenate*. (New York: William H. Sadlier, Inc., 1979), pp. 52-53. This book is a pastor's reflections upon several years experience implementing the RCIA; it is the best book I know for walking parish ministers through the rite.

34 Colman McCarthy, *Inner Companions*. (Washington, DC: Acropolis Books, 1975), p. 18.

35 Ralph Keifer, in *Liturgy 70*, 8:8, p. 9.

36 Aidan Kavanagh, *The Shape of Baptism: the Rite of Christian Initiation*. (New York: Pueblo Publishing Co., 1978), p. 190.

37 Kemp, *A Journey in Faith*, p. 59.

38 The clearest presentation of Fowler's theses that I have seen is in his dialogue with Sam Keen in *Life Maps: Conversation about the Journey of Faith*. (Waco, TX: Word Publications, 1978); Keen begins by accusing Fowler (and Kohlberg) of being too cognitive and not sufficiently affective; Fowler protests that he is affective, and they both end agreeing with great affection.

39 Virgil Elizondo, "The Catechumenate in the Hispanic Community," in *Becoming a Catholic Christian*. (New York: William H. Sadlier, Inc., 1978), pp. 43, 44.

40 Kavanagh, *The Shape of Baptism*, p. 168: also cf. Kemp, *A Journey in Faith*, pp. 74-82 for qualities of the catechists.

41 Michel Dujarier and Theophile Villaca, "The Various Ministries of Christian Initiation," In *Becoming a Catholic Christian*. (New York: William H. Sadlier, Inc., 1978), pp. 136-137.

42 cf. Kemp, *A Journey in Faith*, pp. 55-57, for comments on sponsors.

43 Charles Gusmer, "How Do Liturgists View Initiation?", in *Christian Initiation Resources*, Vol. 1, pp. 14-19.

44 Michel Dujarier, "A Survery of the History of the Catechumenate," in *Becoming a Catholic Christian*. (New York: William H. Sadlier, Inc., 1978), pp. 10-11.

45 cf. Kemp, *A Journey in Faith*, pp. 66-73 for suggestions for the liturgies.

46 For a treatment of demons in our times, cf. Gregory Baum's section on the demonic in *Man Becoming: God in Secular Language*. (New York: Herder and Herder, 1970), pp. 118-126.

47 Greeley translates the questions of the Baltimore Catechism into human life, ultimate questions.

48 P. Faugere, *Pensees, fragments et lettres de Blaise*, Paris, 1897.

49 Walter Conn, editor, *Conversion: Perspectives on Personal and Social Transformation*. (New York: Alba House, 1978).

50 Bernard Cooke, *Ministry to Word and Sacraments: History and Theology*. (Philadelphia: Fortress Press, 1976).

51 Kenneth Boyack offers questions which form the basis of a personal interview with the candidate before the Rite of Election, in *A Parish Guide to Adult Initiation*, p. 65.

52 Maurice Dingman, "The Role of the Bishop . . .", p. 144

53 Bishop Dingman adds pastoral suggestions for bishops, *Ibid.*, pp. 149-52.

54 Kavanagh, *The Shape of Baptism*, pp. 186, 187.

55 Kemp, *A Journey in Faith*, p. 129.

56 James Parker, "The Stages of Initiation, III. Purification and Enlightenment," in *Becoming A Catholic Christian*. (New York: William H. Sadlier, Inc., 1978), p. 118.

57 Parker, "The Stages . . .", pp. 119-120.

58 Parker, "The Stages . . .", p. 120.

59 Catherine de Vinck, *A Passion Play*. (Allendale, NJ: Alleluia Press.)

60 Thomas Downs, *A Journey to Self Through Dialogue: An excursion of self-discovery for individuals and groups*. (West Mystic, CT: Twenty-third Publications, 1977), p. 66.

61 John Costanzo, "The Sacred Heart Project," *New Catholic World*. 222:1329, p. 187.

62 Kavanagh, *The Shape of Baptism*, p. 179.

63 For a more extended treatment of functions of the right and left lobe, especially regarding implications for liturgy, cf. Gerald Lardner, "Evaluative Criteria and the Liturgy," *Worship*, Sept. 1979, pp. 357-369.

64 Joseph Gelineau, "The Symbols of Christian Initiation," in *Becoming a Catholic Christian*. (New York: William H. Sadlier, Inc., 1978), p. 181.

65 Albert Benavides, "An Experience of a Large Urban Mexican American Parish," in *Becoming a Catholic Christian*. (New York: William H. Sadlier, Inc., 1978), p. 56.

66 For addittional suggestions concering the period of mystagogia, cf. Kemp, *A Journey in Faith*, pp. 155-167, and my paper, "The Stages of Initiation IV. The Sacraments of Initiation and Afterward," in *Becoming a Catholic Christian*. (New York: William H. Sadlier, Inc., 1978), pp. 125-131.

67 I have recently written a book that helps people discern their Christian service and ministries, cf. James B. Dunning, *Ministries: Sharing God's Gifts*. (Winona, MN: St. Mary's Press, 1980).

68 Alice Meynell cited by John Costanzo, "The Sacred Heart Project..." p. 187.

69 In *Made, Not Born*. (Notre Dame: University of Notre Dame Press, 1976).

70 Kavanagh, "Initiation," in *Simple Gifts*, Vol. II.

71 For reflections on infant baptism, cf. Edward Braxton, "Adult Initiation and Infant Baptism," in *Becoming a Catholic Christian*. (New York: William H. Sadlier, Inc., 1978), pp. 162-177; and Brain Haggarty, "Adult Initiation and Infant Baptism," *New Catholic World*, 222:1329, pp. 157-160.

72 John Roberto, "Confirmation in the American Catholic Church," *The Living Light*, 15:2, pp. 278-279.

73 Ralph Keifer, in *Liturgy 70*, special issue on the RCIA, p. 9.

74 William A. Bauman, "An Experience of an Urban Parish in the Midwest," in *Becoming a Catholic Christian*. (New York: William H. Sadlier, Inc., 1978), pp. 49-53.